With all my love. 179/88.
Fredk

From

The W
34 Great Sutton S

Caesarina Kona Makhoere was born and brought up in South Africa. She was active in the black students' resistance to Bantu education in 1976, and as a result was imprisoned for six years. After her release she worked for the Black Sash organisation as an advice worker for people charged with breaking pass laws, or threatened with discrimination at work. She has worked in the cultural department of the African National Congress, and is currently studying for a business degree.

Caesarina Kona Makhoere

No Child's Play

In prison under apartheid

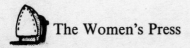 The Women's Press

First published by The Women's Press Ltd 1988
A member of the Namara Group
34 Great Sutton Street, London EC1V 0DX

Copyright © Caesarina Kona Makhoere 1988

British Library Cataloguing in Publication Data

Makhoere, Caesarina Kona
  No child's play.
  1. South Africa. Black women prisoners.
  Treatment — Biographies
  I. Title
  365'.43'092'4

  ISBN 0-7043-4111-5

Typeset by AKM Associates (UK) Ltd,
Ajmal House, Hayes Road, Southall, London
Printed and bound by Cox & Wyman, Reading, Berks

Acknowledgments

Thanks to the African National Congress and its Department of Arts and Culture for their tireless assistance in the publication of this book; Judy Seidman, whose friendship, patience, hard work, generosity and direction inspired and birthed *No Child's Play*; Themba Miya, Gladys Tibane, Puleng Boikanyo, Ma Holeboge Machele and Mawela Tladi whose encouragement and full support helped to turn the manuscript into a book; and to Mme Ruth, ausi Barbara and 'Commissar' who opened the doors.

The Freedom Charter

We, the people of South Africa, declare for all our country and the world to know:

That South Africa belongs to all who live in it, black and white, and that no government can justly claim authority unless it is based on the will of the people –

That our people have been robbed of their birthright to land, liberty and peace by a form of government founded on injustice and inequality –

That our country will never be prosperous or free until all our people live in brotherhood, enjoying equal rights and opportunities –

That only a democratic state, based on the will of all the people, can secure to all their birthright without distinction of colour, race, sex or belief –

And therefore, we the people of South Africa, black and white together equals, countrymen and brothers adopt this FREEDOM CHARTER. And we pledge ourselves to strive together, sparing neither strength nor courage, until the democratic changes here set out have been won.

1 The people shall govern

2 All national groups shall have equal rights

3 The people shall share in the country's wealth

4 The land shall be shared among those who work it

5 All shall be equal before the law

6 All shall enjoy equal human rights

7 There shall be work and security

8 The doors of learning and culture shall be opened

9 There shall be houses, security and comfort

10 There shall be peace and friendship

One

In a family of seven children I was the fourth, with four brothers and two sisters. My eldest brother, Moses, died in 1977 aged 29 while I was still in prison. Mokhele, the youngest of my brothers, passed away recently. My sister was killed in a car accident in Potchefstroom at the age of 5 in 1959.

When I was born in 1955 my father had been a policeman for seven years. He was one of those people who got along well with others – a simple man, respected by most people in our neighbourhood. Though a policeman, he was never isolated by the people. Most weekends he spent attending neighbourhood functions. People did not fear him because he was in the police force. He was everybody's friend, even the villains respected him. Today if you ask people about him, they compare him to today's police who are brutal, hardened and lost. He concerned himself less with politics, though. At times he would look at me, shake his head, and say, 'I'm always expecting a white policeman to say, "Come and pick up your daughter's body." ' Irrespective of that, though, he never said, 'Don't do it.'

He knew I was on the streets, organising and fighting, opposing the system. He knew I was in the leadership in the fight against Bantu education in particular, and the anti-apartheid struggle in general.

Even today I don't really blame him for everything that happened to me. He never deliberately tried to hurt me or my mother. He was trapped and could not help pointing out where I was hiding when I was on the run.

Even when I was detained my father used to come round daily, trying to soothe me, to comfort me, saying: 'Don't worry, my child. You know you didn't commit any crime. They must have at least some exhibit, some proof. I don't think they have any proof whatsoever. So I do not see you going to prison.' He repeated this throughout my trial. He tried to get me out on bail but this was refused. He suffered a lot of mental torture. There he was, visiting

1

me, yet he was the one responsible for my being behind bars. He couldn't look me in the eye. Had he not been a policeman, I still think that I would not have been behind bars. He always tried to explain how he was trapped into pointing out my hideout. He was always stammering and at times seemed so lost for words that I couldn't comprehend what he was trying to say to me. I thought he was losing his mind. He would explain that one of the reasons for his actions was the fact that he had only a few months to go before getting his pension and he would have had to forfeit that. He looked really pathetic.

When I was sentenced to five years he was so shocked. He cried like a baby, unashamedly. That was the last day I saw him alive, the last picture of my father I carried to prison. My mother told me afterwards that he was never the same again. I didn't see him again. He died a few months later.

My mother worked for a white family as a domestic servant and spent most of her time slaving for them. She was allowed only one day off every second Sunday. Every day she left home before sunrise and came back tired at sunset when it became dark; she was in no position to look after us. She was in no position to know what we were doing during the day. We had to look after ourselves and that created problems for us children. With no proper guidance we did whatever we liked; thus at 16, I became a mother.

When I was 17 I went back to school to continue my education after arranging with my mother to look after my child. My loving mother had left her work to help me continue my education, by looking after my son. Her death four months after my release from prison, after I had served five years, left me stunned and very sad indeed, for she was my life.

My father wanted one of my older brothers to join him in the police force, but he refused, telling him that he had already applied for a job as a teacher and that that was his life's ambition. They had many arguments. One day my father came back from work with application forms and shoved them into my brother's hands, telling him to fill them in right away. Avoiding an argument, he filled in the application forms without a word. My father threatened to throw him out of the house if he did not join the police force. When the call-up came for my brother to join the police in the next two days, he silently left our home for good. This brought some unpleasantness into the family. My mother cried, blaming my father for forcing his will on us to decide our future.

2

Lady Selbourne was one of the old Pretoria townships where my parents were tenants on a plot of land belonging to Mr Chauke. It was a one-roomed house serving as kitchen, dining-room, bedroom, everything a house is supposed to have. We used a common water tap and toilet that served forty people living in that plot. In the late 1950s we were moved by government authorities to Mamelodi, a township far from the town. By then many townships had been built outside Pretoria for blacks, to further enforce the Group Areas Act.*

Most houses in Mamelodi are four-roomed. They consist of two bedrooms, a kitchen and a dining-room. The water taps and toilet are outside at the back. The houses are small; they do not comply with the Freedom Charter where it says: 'There shall be houses, security and comfort.' There is no comfort in these tinny matchbox houses. Only the main streets were tarred. Recreational facilities were non-existent. During the weekends or school holidays we played in the dusty streets, because even the yards were too small.

My parents were devoted Christians. My mother conducted Sunday school classes at my home whenever she was off-duty. We kids just loved going to church or Sunday school. We just loved it. This helped to take us off the streets.

The architects of Bantu education made it a law that no black child should be accepted for schooling under seven years of age. I was no exception to that rule. To enter secondary school we had to pass standard six and I had to take it twice. It is hard to pass this standard six, deliberately hard, because of the inferior education of Bantu schools.

When I left my child in the loving care of my mother to continue my education I was 17 years old. I joined Vlakfontein Technical High School in 1972. Two thirds of the teaching staff, including the principal and his deputy, were white soldiers from the South African Defence Force (SADF) appointed by the powers that be. Of the two-thirds five were English-speaking and the rest were Afrikaans-speaking teachers. These teachers were unqualified and co-opted into the Bantu education system as instruments of the regime's policies. So they brought the most virulent racism into our schools. For instance, there was a staffroom for white teachers

*The 1950 Group Areas Act designated areas as White, Coloured, Indian, Black. People were restricted to these areas for residency, owning property or starting a business. When Johannesburg was declared a white area, many Africans were forcibly moved to Soweto. The Act is still in effect.

only, which had a clean, decent appearance. Even their toilets were sparkling clean. They had hired an old black man to keep them clean. The black teachers used a separate staffroom which was dark, very small and uncared for. They had to look after their own staffroom – because the principal did not allow the old man to look after it.

There was one white teacher who used to call us 'apes'. This would infuriate us and we told the principal – who just grunted and dismissed our complaint.

The introducton of Afrikaans as a medium of instruction by the architects of Bantu education was like putting salt on an existing wound. Was it not enough to let us swallow the poisonous education they were pushing down our throats? Now they wanted us to be fluent Afrikaans speakers. We said 'no' to that.

Blacks seriously revolted when Bantu education was introduced in the fifties. Many black schools were started by progressive groups in the country, but the racist regime closed them. Blacks get the lowest standard of education with a very limited scope. This creates serious problems for us after leaving school because we are the last to be hired and the first to be fired. All this is done with the blessing of the government, which has the audacity to decide what it thinks is good and bad for us. As blacks we are never consulted when they make these inhumane laws.

At no stage did they listen to our demands. Students in Soweto started rejecting Afrikaans as a medium of instruction at the beginning of January 1976. Teaching in Afrikaans was supposed to begin in January when the first term of the year starts. To show their rejection of Afrikaans, students refused to go to classes, and their demand was legitimate. As usual, the apartheid regime did not bother to attend to the problem. The demonstrations started with one school and spread to others; by June a good number of schools were already boycotting classes.

A peaceful march was organised by Soweto students. The 'security forces' (police and special army units) answered the peaceful march with bullets, killing many students. Little Hector Peterson, aged 13, was the first victim. Several others were wounded. All hell broke loose. The riots that took place there became a spark that ignited the whole country.

The deputy minister of Bantu education then had the gall to say 'We build schools for them, we pay their teachers, we know what is good for them.' That made us very angry at our school on 17 June 1976. Anger was on every student's face and there was serious

4

tension. Students were gathering in small groups and the Soweto killings were the centre of discussion. We felt we were part of the murdered, wounded and arrested, we were one, they were our brothers and sisters. Their refusal of Afrikaans as a medium of instruction was correct.

The demonstrations on 21 June 1976 all over Pretoria were acts of solidarity with the fallen in Soweto. The racist regime had proved to us that it did not value our lives. We decided to burn down all the racist institutions that symbolised apartheid. Mamelodi was in flames and that was the only way we could show our bitterness.

The white teachers from our school were escorted out of the township by a heavy police escort – this shows how highly their lives were valued!

A few days later, as the flames became more sporadic, we went back to school and our classes, in response to pleas from our parents and the student leaders. Otherwise we would have gone on into Pretoria, and burned down the white monuments of apartheid.

One day in the school yard, during break, we were standing around in groups. The police came, drew their guns and started shooting. Just like that. They started shooting without any provocation whatsoever. We all ran into the classrooms. Two school mates didn't make it; they lay there, in the yard, wounded.

The principal left his office, followed by the vice-principal, and walked to the injured students. They both helped the students to their feet and led them to the waiting police and handed them over. We were shocked. This man had handed our fellow students to the waiting police! We were very angry. We spilled out of the classrooms. Some of the students started to pick up stones, but the student leaders warned them against throwing them. The police were telling the principal to order us to go home, to leave the school premises immediately. The principal did. We left with no further incident.

The following day we assembled in the school yard, but only the black teachers were present. One black teacher told us that he had been instructed to tell us that the school was closed until further notice. That made us angry once more. We went to other schools, urging the students to boycott classes as the police were taking over, and we told the students of these schools to join our protest. The slogan we chanted was: 'Close one, close all.' All the Mamelodi schools were closed that day.

5

There were riots for the whole week; beer halls were burnt, municipal vehicles were looted and burnt, administration offices were stoned and burnt; there were many running battles with the police and some children were shot and taken away. After a week things cooled down.

Parents and student leaders urged us to go back to school. We agreed and went back. We were still angry but we played it cool. When the bell rang we all assembled in the school yard. But when the teachers appeared, standing in front of us, we charged at them. We were angry because these very white teachers had handed over our wounded colleagues to the police to be arrested. By beating them up we wanted to show them how we had no respect for them, that we were not afraid of them. We had stopped being nice, tolerant, obedient students. This was the language they understood best.

This act of course accelerated the riots again. I was not sleeping at home some nights but organising and urging the comrades, taking the wounded to hospital, holding meetings at secret places. Those whose homes were raided by the police we sent underground. The killing and butchering of students never stopped. This called for urgent decisions. The shooting of students, the atrocities done to the people, the thousands of people sent to prisons, made us come to one conclusion: we had to adopt armed struggle.

You can't fight bullets with stones. The trigger-happy apartheid monster had to be met with its own death weapon. Period. End violence by violence, period. It was better to send our comrades outside to be trained and armed. It was time for our comrades to rise and join our only shield: *Umkhonto We Sizwe* (The Spear of the Nation), the military wing of the African National Congress, known as MK.

I spoke to seven people, six of them students. I wanted us to get military training. Unfortunately one of our committee members was arrested and revealed all our plans and those we had carried out. The place was now very hot for me. We had to hide. I decided to go to my relative in Potchefstroom and lie low for a bit. That was the biggest mistake I have ever made.

On the eleventh day, while hiding, I saw my father approaching with two other men. When they came into the house my father told me that they were from the police and they had come to arrest me. That was 25 October 1976.

Two

I spent a night at Mamelodi Police Station. The following day I was taken to Compol Building in the centre of town. Compol Building houses the Pretoria Security Police. I was marched to the first floor, into a small room where, without warning, I was beaten up. Four hefty men, two white and two black, gave me the beating of my life. Van der Merwe, Beukes, Selepe and Dunura threw me all over the place. I thought they would kill me there and then. All the time Selepe was screaming at me, cursing me all the time. Then they took their jackets off and the interrogation began. Selepe was the most vicious, a sadist. He screamed at me: 'You will not get out of here alive if you don't co-operate! Do you hear? I have dealt with political upstarts like you before. I can kill you and think nothing of it – the law is protecting me. Just tell us what we want then everything will be all right for you. If you don't we will force it out of you.' A big, very black, policeman, threatening and boasting to a defenceless young woman.

Of course, I denied everything they asked and accused me of. Van der Merwe became red in the face, accusing me of not being co-operative, and he ordered Selepe to continue beating me up. When Selepe heard the order he dived at me and started throwing punches all over my body. It's always the same when white and black policemen work together on a case; the black policeman hits you the hardest in front of his white superiors; he throws his weight behind every punch and every kick leaves scars on your body. Just to show his white superior how much he despises you. I suppose it is guilt that makes them so much more vicious than their white counterparts. Everyone interrogated between 1976 and 1977 knows how vicious Selepe was. When a unit of *Umkhonto We Sizwe* riddled Selepe with bullets, only two weeks after my release in 1982, it was like a ritual offering as a celebration for my release.

The torture was both mental and physical. Beukes was like many Afrikaners. He never saw anything beyond defending the Afrikaans way of life. He saw communists in everyone opposing him on anything. He was convinced that all black schoolchildren were now newly converted communists, and he was out to stamp out communism. I remember one day in the Compol Building during lunch when he said: '*Die bloodie Communiste magt nie eet nie* [Those bloody communists shouldn't be given food]. *Ons kan skaars rus met hulle nonsense* [We can hardly rest because of their nonsense].' I could see he really meant that. He had such hatred within him, he could not hide it. At times he would scream at me, telling me how 'they' would defend 'their' country against communists like us.

The ordeal I underwent still hurts today. Other people have described how helpless you feel, how at some point you no longer know you are human; that's how I felt.

It was not long after this that Mbongeni, a student activist from Soweto, was killed by the security police at another notorious police station, that of the security police section at John Vorster Square in Johannesburg. His death in detention made Selepe so proud.

I had passed by Compol Building so many times, never realising what was happening inside. I vaguely imagined it to be some museum or something; one solid grey government edifice. Ask Steve Biko, wherever he is sleeping now, about that building. Biko, who is still regarded as the father of Black Consciousness in South Africa, was the founder member of the South African Student Organisation (SASO) and the Black People's Convention (BPC). He was in Compol Building in the hands of the security police before he died.

Every day after interrogation I was taken to Pretoria Central Prison which is situated on the western side of Pretoria. It is about one kilometre from the SADF Barracks. The building is a nightmare. It was a government mortuary before it was converted into a prison. This is where people who are sentenced to death are hanged, and where most white political prisoners are kept.

On arrival that first day I was taken to the reception. A good number of white wardresses were busy with their office work, a black wardress was on sentry duty and two others seemed afraid, as if warned not to look at me. When I was brought in, all the white wardresses stopped working for a while and looked at me, as if I had just landed from the moon. After they had satisfied their curiosity they went back to their work and forgot about me.

After particulars were taken, one of the wardresses, whom I later learned was the head of the prison in the women's section, ordered

8

an elderly wardress to strip me and search my belongings. A thorough search was done of my clothes and I was ordered to open my mouth, put my hands up, and spread my legs apart. She found nothing and ordered me to dress. The door of the room was locked. I was alone. Thus began my solitary confinement.

The room consisted of a water bucket, a pot to relieve myself into, a thick mat, three blankets, a small metal container for water, and a small window that brought in light. Through this small window I could see a grey wall, but nothing beyond that. When it was hot during the day the room smelt like hell; even the disinfectant did not work because I could only empty the pot in the morning. I also had my meals in this room. There was no reading material, nothing whatsoever to keep me busy. I was given fifteen minutes or less for my bath and another half-hour for exercising in the yard. I spent exercise time walking around the yard.

The elderly wardress who had brought me into the cell was the one responsible for everything connected with me. She was in her fifties and a bit greyish at the temples. Of medium height, stout and with brown eyes. A pension would do her good. She must have been in the prison department all her life. If she left this job she would have nowhere to go.

The prison head was an aloof type, a real snob. She was in her early thirties, of medium height, slender and fair skinned. She wouldn't let anyone forget that she was the head of the prison. Whenever she talked to me she wanted me to stand up with my hands behind my back. She always wanted me to show obedience. A complaint about food to her was a fruitless exercise. She always reminded me that this was not my home and not a hotel.

During that period it was clear that the white prison staff had little trust for their black colleagues, because they never worked in a section where political prisoners and detainees were locked up. They worked only in the petty offenders' section. They were not even allowed to speak to political prisoners.

Black prisoners were hidden whenever I was supposed to go out of the cell. If they appeared when I was led out they were shooed away before they could even see me.

On 13 January 1977 I was transferred to Silverton Police Station only fifteen kilometres from Mamelodi. The building had red bricks, and was surrounded by a beautiful flower garden maintained by short-term prisoners. The double-storey building consisted of reception, administration offices and various others which I knew nothing about. The cells were right at the back, about forty metres from the double-storey building inside the yard. There were two blocks of cells, each containing four cells. Next to one of the blocks was a parking bay for the warders' cars. About three hundred metres from the cells was the station commander's house.

After all my particulars had been taken I was shown into my cell, a cell I was to occupy for the next four months. This had a flushing toilet inside the cell and a courtyard in front of the cell of the same size. In this courtyard there was a shower with only cold running water and a wash basin next to it. There was mesh fence at the top.

All the white police had a negative attitude towards me, but surprisingly the black and coloured police were sympathetic. They would give me courage by saying: 'One day we shall overcome, sister.' They always turned a blind eye when some of the prisoners gave me a share of the meat which had been smuggled into the gaol. Almost all the prisoners serving sentences in this police station stood by me. All of this gave me courage.

I ate stiff maize (mealie) porridge three times a day with plain water, except for the times I ate the smuggled meat. I thought Pretoria Central Prison was terrible, but at least there I had eaten meat three times a week. The station commander, a middle-aged clean-shaven Afrikaner with dark hair and neatly dressed, came every morning asking for complaints. This was just a formality, because nothing was done after I had complained.

I was a detainee left in a cell alone. Always alone, except for when I was being interrogated. Life was very tough then; I was sleeping on the floor and developed a heart problem. A magistrate visited me fortnightly on Fridays. I lodged a lot of complaints with him, but he seemed not to take them seriously because things remained exactly the same.

To keep myself sane I used to sing religious songs, protest songs and even folk songs. As my cell was sandwiched between two other cells I could hear footsteps coming and going. If they unlocked the door of the first cell, I would know there had to be people in there. A few minutes after they had locked up I would bang on the wall with both my feet and hands. I would bang until they hurt and the other detainees would respond by also banging on their side of the wall. That would excite me so! The windows had a mesh wire with a small hole between the wire where one could open the window. I would open the window and shout a greeting to the prisoner next door who had just responded to my banging, and she would shout a greeting back through the window. We would talk about anything, anything under the sun. Then, when we heard the keys rattling at the main door, we would be silent.

The short-term prisoners, who were permitted to move outside their cells, would creep into the passage and stand against the wall where I could see them. I would stand on top of the toilet seat to be able to see outside; to be able to see their faces while we talked. When I heard the keys, because I could hear the keys from afar, my ears were getting tuned in so well, I would climb off the toilet seat and the prisoner outside would try to look busy. Talking to these prisoners kept me sane, kept me going.

As I said before, I like singing. Some of my time I spent singing, even though singing was prohibited and the station commander was getting worked up about it. He threatened that if I continued with that kind of behaviour he would send me away. I liked that, and started to sing louder. But the station commander, being the coward that he was, did not follow through his threats. I remained.

I stayed in detention under Section 6 of the Security Act of 1967, which allowed the police to keep a person in detention for six months (renewable!) without being charged. I was in detention for more than six months, without appearing in court, not knowing why I had been detained and locked up.

On 9 May 1977 at about two in the afternoon I was taken to Pretoria North Magistrates' Court, by Beukes and Van der Merwe. When I appeared before a magistrate I was charged under Section 2 of the Terrorism Act. I was asked to plead and I pleaded 'not guilty'. I was given an indictment and told I would appear again on 20 May 1977. The indictment was long, with a lot of allegations against me. Amongst the few people who were in court, I hardly saw one person I knew.

I appeared in court many times before the initial hearing, which started on 15 August 1977 and ended on 27 October 1977, a full year after my arrest. During the trial I was at first represented by a lawyer but because of financial difficulties he withdrew in the middle of the case. I continued the case on my own.

My father started attending my trial when I appeared for the second time, and from then on he was there all the time. At times he would bring my mother along. They brought me food to eat and a change of clothes. I always felt good and strong when I saw them in court.

The main charges were:
a)   Recruiting people for military training to overthrow the regime;

11

b) Organising school boycotts;
c) Participating in disturbances on 21 June 1976;
d) Leading an assault on white teachers.

Eleven people testified against me. Nine were blacks from Mamelodi and two were whites from the 'immigration' office. They all painted an ugly picture of my young life. They came to prove that I had recruited others to leave the country for military training, and the two whites tried to prove that I had myself taken out a travel document around July or August. They just came and testified that I had applied for a travel document, which I received around that time. Among the state witnesses there was a policeman's daughter, who really disappointed me after I had trusted her so much, as she had befriended me and I had confided in her as a friend.

The other person who let me down was the Right Reverend Lekgotlo, who testified twice against me. I was really disappointed in him. All along I had thought that he understood our sufferings. He gave his damaging testimony, even though I said he had committed perjury. He came again, this time emphasising the fact that I was organising people to leave the country to undergo military training. He did not bat an eyelid when giving this 'evidence'.

I was found guilty only on the charge of recruiting people for military training, not guilty on the rest of the charges. When giving judgment the magistrate relied mainly on Reverend Lekgotlo's evidence. He said, 'I do not expect a Reverend to tell lies. I believe what the Reverend told the court about how you recruited people for military training outside the country. He came here twice testifying against the accused. It is clear proof that the accused committed this crime. What the Reverend says goes hand in hand with what the other witnesses said.'

I was sentenced to five years. When I looked back at the audience, I saw my father crying like a baby, supported by my distraught mother who hung on to him, leading him out of the courtroom.

Three

After conviction, I was taken to Pretoria Central Prison, nick-named 'Lock'. When I was led into this prison the head was very excited to see me with a five-year sentence hanging round my neck. She gloated over me and said, 'You know five years is such a nice long sentence.' Angrily I retorted, 'No. That's you, gloating over me. Today it is me who is going to serve five years but tomorrow it's possible you will also get five years, for the very same type of thing I was convicted for.'

She ordered that I be taken to a cell and searched. I was stripped and also ordered to take off my panties. I felt insulted and asked, 'What for? Why should I take off my panties?' I refused. They did not insist. I got dressed again and was taken to another cell. I slept there and was woken up early in the morning. It was 28 October 1977. I was instructed to take my belongings because I was going somewhere else. I did not know, and I did not ask, where I was to be taken.

In the reception I found two men waiting for me. I learnt later that one of them was Du Plessis, the Brigadier responsible for all political prisoners. He was hated by all the prisoners who had passed through his hands. He was nasty, cruel and racist. He seemed to belong to that group that would rather die than see blacks sharing power. He had it in his mind that blacks were devils and whites, especially Afrikaners, were the chosen children of God and that South Africa was the promised land. That's how brainwashed he was. He tried several times to break our wills by many vile ways. He stopped us from getting visits. Mama Dorothy Nyembe, I knew, had stayed for years in prison without a visit. Such a thing affects a person's mind, and yet Mama Dorothy and all the other comrades managed to keep up their strength. The prison department acted like that deliberately, particularly this Du Plessis. He was in his late fifties, with a pot belly and of medium height. He contributed to the bad behaviour of warders and wardresses. He openly egged them on to be cruel to prisoners.

13

He handcuffed my wrists behind my back. The two men escorted me, marching out with me. Both men were armed with pistols. Later a wardress joined us, following behind. We got into a car with the wardress seated next to me and with both men in front. We then drove to Leeukop Prison in Sandton, not far from Johannesburg. There we picked up another warder and drove straight to Kroonstad Prison in the Orange Free State. This was to be my home for a long time.

In Kroonstad I was subjected to the same treatment I had received before. I was stripped and searched by Warrant Officer Smith, the person responsible for political prisoners. I was never out of sight of my escorts, and I was handcuffed all the way. What did they expect me to do? How stereotyped prison regulations can be.

The physical conditions of Kroonstad were supplemented by the staff. Warrant Officer Smith was a real bitch. She was a bully, clumsy, and most of the time when she came to work she was drunk. She believed her juniors should idolise her. She was especially on top of the world when her captain was not around. She would prance around like a peacock, ordering everyone around as though she owned the whole prison. We prisoners were worst off with her. She would look at us as if we were things coughed up and splashed against a dirty wall. A black person was not expected to talk back to her. Blacks were supposed to shuffle around and nod their heads all the time, but they had to jump when she called. She hated political prisoners most of all. Not suprisingly, she was a product of Brigadier Du Plessis.

There was Captain Callitz, who must be the most stupid person I have ever come across. A tall Afrikaner woman, she kept repeating again and again that there were rules and regulations to be observed. I'm sure she even repeated this in her sleep. No matter how you would try to look for reason from her – you wouldn't get it. That's the kind of fool I was trapped with for my entire stay in Kroonstad Prison.

Then there was Erasmus Junior, whom we used to call Tomboy. She was another fool. She just could not reason. She would start, 'Whatever I tell you *die kaptein sê julle moet so iets doen* [the captain says you must do it].' We would retort, 'Please, can't you talk straight English? It sounds funny and incomprehensible when you start mixing the languages like that.' Like a fool she would try, 'Well the captain said, the captain said . . . agh! *los julle my* [let me go],' and she'd storm away and leave us laughing. She was one of those people who left school too early in their lives. And all because she failed a standard. In South Africa it seems, a white is not supposed to repeat a standard because every Afrikaner should be born intelligent. So if you have to repeat they chase you away.

Later, there was this wardress that we called Mbomvana. Hey, Thixo! I have never come across such a problem. But this one we dealt with, quite effectively. She was a stout woman who could pass for a rugby scrum-half. Her face and arms were so red, like beetroot, she was blonde and around 23 or 24. I was told she was not married yet and I believed this immediately; who would marry a woman who was so sadistic? But such things do happen in this crazy world; I learned she had a boyfriend who was also a warder in the same prison. It was true! I finally saw the boyfriend. Poor Boer boy. He was as thin as a bean stick. I was afraid to imagine how she would throw him around in her fits of anger. Whew!

And of course there was the head of the prison, Brigadier Venter. He is hard to describe. He was a diplomatic, maybe even a cunning person. He was so tactful; he agreed with most of the complaints we raised against his staff and usually promised to solve any one of our problems. And, honestly, he did. His attitude towards the comrades seemed warm and acceptable. He always tried to put himself across as only a servant of the government and promised that if he could help he would. He said he did not believe in some of the laws; for instance, he would say there was no reason why some human beings should discriminate against other human beings. But, he would go on, he just had no power to do anything about it, the power lay in Pretoria. If he was able to change some of the things he would try to do so, but most things he could not change. Of all the prison staff members, he was the one most of the comrades would speak to and be open with. And they would get satisfactory answers, of course – given that they would have to understand that at this stage action would be beyond his powers. When the staff behaved badly towards prisoners, he would stop them and even remove them from the section. Being head of the whole prison he worried about his good record, I suppose.

Brigadier Venter was in his fifties, about six foot tall, hefty, with brown hair, hazy blue eyes and a handsome face. His manners towards people gained him a lot of respect. He regarded other people as human beings, with the result that whatever he said was not lightly taken. At no stage did he use an iron hand towards a prisoner; instead he preferred to talk to and understand a person.

15

At times we would realise that he was forced by his seniors to be a bit hard.

I was taken to the political section. I found Mrs Aminah Desai, Mama Dorothy Nyembe, Mrs Edith Ndala, Mrs Joyce Mashama and Ms Esther Maleka. They said: 'Feel at home. *A luta continua.*'

It was a nice welcome, seeing people like Mama Dorothy who was just about to finish eight-and-a-half years of her 15-year sentence. You know, I thought, if people are able to stay strong for this length of time, five years is just child's play. My introduction to the struggle was the 1976 student demonstrations, then arrest, interrogation, and sentence. But Mama Dorothy had had a very long experience. She had joined the struggle 30 years ago – now, lately, kids begin when they are very young indeed, but in those days it was not so straightforward. Mama Dorothy was recruited when she was 17, by Chief Luthuli himself, the late President of the African National Congress (ANC) of South Africa, and predecessor to comrade President Reginald Oliver Tambo. She organised in Natal in the days when the ANC was legal, in the early days of the Federation of South African Women (FEDSAW). This was the time when people resisted by burning their passes, when thousands of Defiance Campaign volunteers resisted peacefully and went to prison.

I had not known much about FEDSAW, about the women's struggle in our history, before I came to Kroonstad. But Mama Dorothy's stories inspired me. The march to Pretoria, with 20,000 women refusing to accept the law making women carry passes, must have been a very exciting event. And Mama Dorothy participated, knew the courage of these women, these mothers who said no to the evils of the pass laws. Mama Dorothy was one of them. She went to prison in 1969, with a 15-year sentence, the longest sentence a woman has ever served for political offences. She had helped MK soldiers, giving them shelter. Her uncle, Chief Gatsha Buthelezi, gave evidence against her at her trial, evidence which sent her to prison.

Mama Dorothy is a very strong woman, brave, with convictions which I have to respect highly. She is very quiet and talks very little. If you wanted her to talk you had to start a discussion about politics and religion. Her quietness was once misunderstood by a state witness in her trial, when he told the court that Mama Dorothy was 'a deep crook'. That was Thembinkosi who paraded as 'Mr X' and was later assassinated by MK guerrillas. This lost soul had at some stage worked with Mama Dorothy. This great woman had spent most of her time in this prison reading what she called 'The Good Book', the bible.

The prison tried to break her, but without success. All the time I was at Kroonstad Prison, I never once saw her receiving visitors, not once. Yet she never complained. Communication with her people had broken down some time long before I came to this prison. She had a daughter who was married and had children of her own: two sons. I blame the system for all this. According to their so-called rules and regulations, the Prisons Department is supposed to encourage communication between prisoners and their families. They never ever did that for her, not once. But Mama Dorothy coped with it so well. It can break a weaker person – not even getting a letter. Whenever she talked to me, I felt the warm, soothing words of hope and the spirit of perseverance that goes with the will to live. I would part with her by saying, 'Mama Dorothy, *a luta*, we are taking over when you retire,' and I'd walk away much stronger.

I came in as they were delivering the food for lunch; I was shown directly to my room. Aaaaaiee, I could not believe it. Here was a bed, with sheets and a pillow, a cupboard; here was a toilet, a basin. At least it was an improvement on Pretoria Prison, where you only had a pot, when you go to take a wash you stay with the bad odour all in the room, getting stale, the whole room smelling. At least in this room I would be able to flush my stools away. At least I would be able to get fresh water.

Mama Aminah said, 'You know, Caesarina, I think you are fortunate compared to us. You know, when we were at Barberton Prison we had it very tough. There was no bed, there was nothing. And you might think you were visiting your uncle's place here, with beds and everything.' I was incensed. Imagine telling a newly arrived with a five-year sentence that she is lucky!

Aminah Desai was arrested in 1971, together with Ahmed Timol, one of the first political detainees to die in the hands of the police at John Vorster Square. She was found guilty of breaking the Terrorism Act in January 1974 and was sentenced to five years after a long stay in detention. She is the mother of four children, three daughters and a son. They are all grown up and in exile. She was in her late fifties, quiet, withdrawn, though a very warm personality even in the most trying of times. She used to laugh her problems away as if they were not so serious. After her sentence she was taken to Barberton Prison in the Eastern Transvaal where she joined Mama Dorothy, before they were both transferred to

Kroonstad. As a Muslim she adhered strictly to her religion, observing all its rules. She was released in January 1978 after spending seven years inside without remission.

When I came to Kroonstad Prison, it was divided into sections, although we exercised in the same big yard. In one section Mama Dorothy and Mama Aminah stayed together; this is where I too was accommodated. Mama Edith, ausi (sister) Joyce and ausi Esther stayed together in the big section. Each night they locked us into our single cells, alone. But during the day we were together. If the apartheid gods who rule us tried to break us, being comrades together gave us courage.

When I came out, I knew I had a lot to do. Outside I would be telling the comrades we had to start reorganising ourselves. That the seeds of revolution have bloomed. It is now time to go to the market place. Period. It was because of Mama Dorothy and all the other sisters whose contributions are still unsurpassed. The pillars of the struggle have always been the women, even though we were never given the accolades we deserved. We have to do it now and leave a strong heritage for future generations. We have to carry the flag of the sisters high.

And all the other sisters resisting inside the prisons, who were my strength when times were hard – here I'm talking about aus Joyce, aus Esther and Thandisa – deserve special mention together with Mama Dorothy. They fought an inimitable war in the dungeons of the hellish racists. We fought inside the cold, damp walls that kept us locked in, away from our fathers and mothers, husbands, sisters, brothers and children who are on the streets taking and giving hell to the military monster that is waging war to preserve its ugly past. We, the people, fighting for a glorious future for the beauty of all. But now I'm talking about the sisters who threw away the kitchen apron for cold steel in their hands – the hands which are capable of caressing and loving, oh so well.

Four

The prisons gave us work to do like ironing and crocheting. I was expected to iron, together with Mama Dorothy. To be honest, I did not know whose clothes they were, and that made me angry. They would bring the clothes from the other section of the prison, black prisoners' uniforms, and say: 'Here, this is your amount of work to be ironed today.' They were telling me and Mama Dorothy, and the other four were to do crocheting. Mama Aminah only repeated, 'I don't care whether I'm going to finish this thing after my release or what; I'm just passing time.' In some cases they would bring wet clothes and expect us to dry them. At first I told them, 'Listen, we want to know the procedure. I also want to know crocheting. I'm not going to iron for the rest of my sentence.' And they responded, 'Don't worry. We are going to make arrangements.' But the original set-up continued, and when I complained that these people were continuing to give us ironing, although they had promised we would take turns, they reminded me: 'Don't forget, you are a prisoner.'

It has always been my tendency to study the situation first, quietly. I don't just attack immediately. Thus in October 1977 I studied the situation. We continued to work through November. Day after day, we worked from eight o'clock to 11 o'clock, then we had lunch. At twenty to twelve, they would lock us up, then unlock us again for work at one. We would work until two o'clock, often we would go for exercise, after exercise we had our supper. They locked us up at three. And it continued like that.

The exercise they expected us to perform was to walk around the yard in circles; they called it exercise. It was just a big yard, with cement walls surrounding it, and a cement pavement skirting the wall, an edge of flower beds, a square lawn in the middle, and one tree, smack in the centre, a peach tree. We decided that peach tree belonged to the people, meaning us. It would bear peaches, golden, round and juicy. And as far as we were concerned the peaches were ours, only. We got no fruit in our official diet. We agreed that black male prisoners who mowed the lawn should take the peaches with the understanding that we were suffering the same fate. But let any white warder or wardress try it and we would scream through the windows: 'Hey! What are you doing? Leave our peaches alone!' Eventually even the wardresses accepted that it was more peaceful to ask our permission to eat those peaches.

Once Mbomvana decided that she would assume control of our beautiful peach tree. We screamed at her. Was she not ashamed, stealing the prisoners' peaches? And we told her to stop it. When she didn't, we lodged a complaint with the captain, to stop Mbomvana stealing from our beautiful peach tree, a full-scale formal complaint which brought down Mbomvana from her high and mighty imaginary perch. She had to ask permission from us, which we often refused, to get near that peach tree. The supervisor in charge of our tree was Mama Dorothy. We gave permission to all prisoners only. We very rarely gave permission to prison officials. Agh, those peaches were nice.

The walls of the exercise yard were something like ten metres high, so there was no point thinking about escaping. You just had to forget about it. Normally at supper time we were locked into the small section first, and the big section would be locked up later. One day, for some reason, Mbomvana went straight to the big section and started to have a friendly chat with Mama Dorothy and Thandisa. After some time she left in a hurry without locking the grille, leaving us outside!

It grew dark. We looked up at the stars. It was the only time in six years in prison that I was able to gaze at the stars. Being outside my cell, standing beneath the stars, dreaming, dreaming of freedom. If only we could climb that wall, if they could find us gone, if we could touch the sky, if . . . We talked about freedom and a possible way out of there. But then there were guards patrolling the prison accompanied by guard dogs. Escaping is always in the prisoner's mind. It's natural, I suppose. You just cannot help dreaming sometimes, can you? But look at the security – maybe it was a trap and they wanted to shoot us. Maybe . . . Oh well, at all events we spent the night beneath the stars.

We were expected to parade daily when we were locked up. You had to stand at attention, inside your cell, about a metre from the grille, with your hands clasped behind you. They were just never too tired to recite or read the prison rules and regulations. At times they did that before lock-up. I was getting annoyed with all this. Nobody had ever consulted us about these rules and regulations when they were planned and made law, anyway.

They gave us clothes, according to some bureaucratic whim of long ago. Each of us had two denim overalls, two *doeks* (turbans), and two pairs of panties. Let me describe the panties. They were baggy white shorts with no elastic where they ended, which was somewhere mid-thigh; they had elastic only at the waist. They were the thick, old-fashioned cotton type. How could the Prisons Department expect us to use pads with that type of panties? They would look very good on soccer players on the field.

Somebody came up with a bright idea. Mama Aminah had varicose veins and they gave her pantie-hose to cover her legs. When these became old (the pantie-hose, that is), instead of throwing them away she would give them to us. We discovered that we could take the elastic from Mama Aminah's pantie-hose and sew them to the legs of the panties so a person could be more comfortable, if not precisely in style.

We were expected to wear men's shoes, solid, clomping tough shoes meant to last for the whole five years. They did not give us any polish for the shoes, either. To round off our wardrobe, we were given two khaki-grey nighties, one with long sleeves, one with short sleeves; V-neck jerseys, two each; men's socks; and a white apron, as well as a red and yellow *doek*. Looking at this ensemble, a normal, reasonable person could see that this was insane. The place looked like a mental asylum when we appeared in these crazy combinations of clothes. White apron, sky-blue denim overalls, navy-blue jersey, brown shoes, navy-blue socks and red *doek*! These people had decided to treat us like mad people, but all identically mad, a uniform insanity.

When it came to white prisoners, things were different. We could see some white prisoners; they were feeling at home. All white prisoners had the chance to choose what type of shoes they wanted. They had stylish shoes and sandals, shoes you might get at Cuthberts or any decent shoe shop in town, and the dresses were all smart. Different dresses they chose; no uniforms for the white ladies. You would not be able to identify any one of them as a prisoner. Also they did not have to wear *doeks* to cover their heads like housemaids. They might have been mistaken for newly employed wardresses or visitors.

And the food again. On Mondays for breakfast we got porridge with weak black coffee or tea. Black, as milk counted as a privilege. The prison staff admitted that they did not know the type of coffee we were drinking. Some of the older women maintained they

21

would take some mealies, *braai* (grill) them, grind them, and boil the grounds to make coffee. The tea was like red *muti* (medicine) that some *nnyangas* (African traditional doctors) use. The prison staff did not know the name of that tea, either. I think this tea made us ill, or perhaps all of the diet made us ill.

At lunchtime we ate mealies (maize), with either rotten cabbage with insects and black spots on it, or carrots cooked until brown in some sort of syrup, and a mug of *phuzamandla*. This is a drink I've only found in prison, and have never seen outside. It is a yellow powder they mix with water and give to the prisoners. They claimed it would make us strong – as the Zulu name *phuzamandla*, meaning drink strength.

And for supper – this is still Monday's food – we were given *somos*, soya beans. Imagine taking the stuff as it is, putting it into a pot, pouring on salt and then serving. I bet the people you are serving might think you are trying to poison them. So we were given *somos* with soft porridge and a slice of bread: bread to us was like cake. And they would give us something made from some brown powder and water which they called soup.

Breakfast was the same all week, the whole month, the whole year through. Maize porridge with either coffee or that *muti* tea. Lunch was the same, except when they changed to *samp* (a form of maize that is only partially grinded rather like what Americans call hominy) on Sundays. And that *samp*, I'm sure they boiled it a little and then served it; it was terrible.

With supper they went to town; Monday was *somos*; Tuesday, fish; Wednesday, meat with a slice of bread; Thursday, *somos* again; Friday, fish; Saturday, *somos*, yet again; Sunday, meat. This was repeated week after week.

Even with that overly familiar menu, the food was prepared in indescribably awful ways. Their recipe for fish, for example: mix it up, bones and all, and put on to boil. Recipe for *somos*: do the same and add salt. They wanted to make life unbearable for us. They would often remind us not to forget that we were prisoners – as if we could forget.

We were three in my section, and the other three comrades stayed in the other section. During breakfast, lunch and supper, each group of three would receive their food together. In our section, Mama Dorothy could not eat mealies or soft porridge. She got bread for breakfast, lunch and supper – four slices. The doctor had prescribed bread for her serious stomach problems. Aminah Desai's diet was completely different. Her breakfast was bread

22

with jam or syrup, coffee or tea with a dash of milk; lunch, bread and well prepared vegetables; supper, mealie rice with meat or fish. She was getting meat three times a week, fish twice a week and *somos* also twice a week. When we questioned her different diet the answer was: 'She is Coloured. So she's getting a Coloured diet.' So it goes without saying that what Aminah Desai ate was considered too good for us blacks.

If you want to find out what racial discrimination is, just go to any South African prison. The reality is very hard. Here are three people sharing the same table. Yet what they eat is divided on racial lines. And you are expected not to be hurt. Mama Aminah has a 'Coloured' diet and Mama Dorothy another different diet, while the four of us – Aus Joyce, Aus Esther, Mama Edith and myself have to eat rubbish food. That was not acceptable to us. We could not let that kind of madness continue unchallenged.

I was a bit fortunate because Mama Dorothy and Mama Aminah always shared their bread with me. At that time, staying with grown-up people, since I was the youngest, I got a little spoiled. Here I was sharing bread with these two beautiful people and yet our other comrades, in the other cell, could not have the same bread we were enjoying. That made me feel bad. Even though at times we managed to leave them some.

This was Kroonstad Prison where I started to serve my sentence in 1977.

Five

In all South African prisons there are grading systems for the entire prison population, including whites. Prisoners are graded in four categories, A, B, C or D, on account of length of stay or behaviour. Group A is the most privileged; Mama Aminah was graded A because she was Coloured and Mama Dorothy because of her long sentence. They were allowed to buy their own groceries, cosmetics and toiletries. Mama Aminah and Mama Dorothy had been resisting inside for years and had never been beaten by the system.

They earned the A grading the hard way – unlike some prisoners who got the A grading because they sold out to the prison staff. With Mama Aminah the system failed to make us see her as different from us. They always tried to remind her that she was not one of us and they also tried to treat her differently, but they failed in the process. They did not break our solidarity.

At Christmas time, in 1977, they told us that we too, not just the A group, could buy something. The amount of food we were permitted to buy was not to exceed 1500 grammes. We bought ourselves some sweets, biscuits and dried fruits. That Christmas I behaved like a baby. I ate my sweets the first day they gave them to me. We had bought the sweets with our own money, the whole six of us. We were given the sweets on Christmas Eve, and I went for them. I just gobbled them up so greedily that in no time at all I had finished them. Mama Dorothy kept warning me, saying, 'Caesarina, don't eat those sweets so fast. You are going to get ill.' I couldn't answer immediately with my mouth full of sweets, and when I could I said, 'Mama Dorothy, I haven't had sweets for such a long time. I can't help gobbling them up.' I threw some more into my mouth and did a good demolition job. Come Christmas morning, I was so ill that they had to nurse me for the whole day. That was my worst Christmas.

You know how these hypocrites take Christmas? They go about telling prisoners all over the country that they don't have to wear prison uniform on Christmas Day. You can put on your own clothes, you can look any way you like, they tell you with a Hollywood smile all over their usually hardened faces. Common law prisoners usually dress up and look smart. They expected us to dress up too. We refused to put our own clothes on. We argued against that, telling them that we did not intend to take as a special Christmas privilege something that we regarded as our right the whole year round. So we refused to put on our own clothes. How could they expect us to put on our own clothes only once a year, as a treat? If they were aware of how much we hated their uniform, let them allow us to wear our own clothes the whole year round then, we argued. We should wear our own clothes every day, all the year round, just like the white prisoners did, not only on Christmas Day.

On 26 December, Mama Aminah was told to pack her things because the following day she was to be moved. She was due to be released in early January – I think it was the sixth. We were so happy for her and she was so sad to leave us behind. We ended up

24

consoling her instead. Next morning she was taken to a Johannesburg prison.

In January 1978 the International Red Cross came to see us. A week beforehand the attitude of the prison staff changed dramatically. Ach, shame, they were so nice. The whole prison was spruced up. Many prisoners wore new uniforms. Everything was up to date. As a recent arrival I didn't know what was happening; my comrades cleared me up on this: 'The International Red Cross must be sending a delegation. That must be why they are behaving like this, the prison wardresses do that.' Then the delegation came. They brought us some chocolate to eat. I quickly gobbled mine up, forgetting how sick I had been on Christmas Day. We lodged quite a number of complaints: about the food, working conditions, reading material, indoor games (we had none) and about the attitude of the wardresses, particularly the one called Smith who wanted to treat us like the undesirables of this world. And many other complaints we had, too. The International Red Cross said they would ask the Prisons Department officials whether they would permit the Red Cross to buy us recreational equipment such as table tennis sets, basket ball, playing cards, Scrabble and Monopoly sets and any other games, just to keep us busy and help keep our minds relaxed. Aus Esther, Aus Joyce and I asked them if they could get us permission from the authorities to study. They agreed. Mama Dorothy was already studying.

As soon as the International Red Cross delegation left, it was back to hell again. They had given us a nice break. But then we felt it was not enough. This neutral stance the Red Cross people claim they are taking sounds false to me. I don't think there is a middle road in this world. How do you become neutral when whole families are wiped out, children are imprisoned, families are removed and dumped in barren lands, armies are sent to occupy black townships, and thousands of people – mostly children – are killed in the angry streets? How can anyone remain neutral in all this madness? You are either with the people or you are with the bullies of this world. The die is cast. Period.

Later we did receive the stuff the Red Cross sent us. We made it a point that when they asked for complaints, which they did every morning, we would demand what the International Red Cross had promised to get us. 'What has happened to it?' we would ask, putting pressure on them. We finally received the stuff in February, even though the prison staff behaved as if the Prisons Department had bought it all for us, and that we were highly privileged to get anything at all.

Aaiiee, then we started to be real chats. We used to do our work in the big section, where Mama Edith, Ausi Esther and Ausi Joyce stayed, because they had ironing boards and a big table there. We liked Scrabble, we were like kids with that game. By this time our stubbornness was building up. And our ears had grown very sharp.

When they brought the clothes in the morning for ironing, we would take the stuff. I would iron the first two shirts and one pair of trousers. Then I'd switch the iron off. And then the four of us – me, Mama Edith, Ausi Esther and Ausi Joyce – would retire to Mama Edith's cell.

One day we decided to play. Scrabble is really interesting and everybody was eager for the whole group of us to be unlocked. We just had to play. The four of us installed ourselves on Mama Edith's bed and got busy with our game. We heard the keys but we were not absolutely sure. Ausi Joyce was sitting next to Mama Edith, who was sitting next to the wall on the bed. Ausi Joyce climbed on top of Mama Edith, then on to the basin to look out of the window. Total disaster! The wardress responsible for the section was there just then. There was confusion – everyone demanding 'Oh Joyce, *manje wenzani?* [what are you doing?]'

Mama Edith remained in her cell to clear things up and we quickly dashed out. Ausi Joyce and Ausi Esther grabbed their crochet work which they had left at the table, and pretended to be working seriously. Meanwhile, I was quickly at the ironing board and ironing a shirt with a stone cold iron. The keys rattled, Smith came in and found us concentrating very hard. Mama Edith flushed her toilet and emerged from her cell. Smith went straight to Mama Edith, handed her a letter, turned around and left. As soon as she left we went back to our Scrabble game.

After Mama Edith's release we realised how much we were going to miss her. We had liked her company very much, her jolly pranks and her outgoing character. The age gap did not matter either to her or to us. A really fine comrade.

When I came to Kroonstad Prison, as I said before, this warrant officer, Smith, was responsible for political prisoners. Her behaviour made it clear that she felt we had to be punished because we had offended the apartheid regime. No one amongst our comrades was on good terms with her.

Back in February, I remember I received two letters from my parents. They had been written in December, but only given to me in February. I found that in these two months she had not let me know that my Mum planned to visit me. She gave me the letters on a Saturday; the next day my Mum came. Smith came walking fast towards my cell and said, 'Prepare yourself, quick come with me – you have a visitor.' Just like that, without warning. Other people were told in advance, so they had time to prepare themselves for their families.

My Mum came with my son; he was then six. They refused me permission to see my own son. They took him into another room, to wait for my Mum under the watchful eye of the white wardress, while I was talking to my mother. In the visiting room there is a glass between the prisoner and the visitor. My Mum and I had to kiss the glass as a greeting. Smith was also in the visiting room about three metres from me. She was listening to our conversation. At times she would interrupt us, stopping us discussing anything to do with politics. The discussion centred around my family, nothing more. After asking how everybody was doing at home I discovered that there was little else we could say to each other, since they had limited the scope of our discussion.

In the meantime my son was singing in the other room. My Mum asked, 'Can you hear his voice?' That small voice was so near and yet so far. I could not take it. My heart was so sore, the pain was so severe. Apartheid, how I hate you, you must be crushed once and for all. You have caused so much pain to human beings. My loving Mum left after thirty minutes. Most of the time we did not know what to say to each other; not that there was nothing to say, it was that apartheid was forbidding us.

Smith was a real nuisance. I had asked for permission to study by a written application as far back as January but come June she had still not given me permission to do so. Time was running out for me. I had been arrested five days before I took my matriculation exam – in South Africa the school leaving and university entrance exam. I now hoped to do it in October and November, final 'matric', that is. In prison I had to buy books, start from the beginning. Fortunately for me it was just revision, but I had not seen books for a year and a half. We could not get books from Kroonstad, we had to buy them COD from Bloemfontein or from commercial suppliers in Johannesburg. And it took time. Even if the books arrived in time, Smith would delay them, keeping them in her office. She held up my books until towards the end of July, some I got only in August. My revision had to be a rushing around, a chaotic thing.

At one stage, I think it was in December 1977, this Smith had very many letters belonging to comrades. We were exercising when she brought out a large pile of letters, our letters, our precious letters. She stood there reading through the pile. We grew excited! Word from home at last! Comrades had not received any letters for about two months, which was something really funny because normally a week wouldn't go by without one of us receiving a letter from home. This time, however, it had been about two months. In the courtyard they kept an incinerator. We watched her dump the whole pile of letters in it, and we watched her light the pile. We watched those letters burn and we felt hopeless. Man, we could taste the bitterness.

This Smith provoked us on many, many, issues. We laid so many complaints against her that Sergeant Erasmus was assigned to us, to the political section, over Smith's head.

Sergeant Erasmus we called Bimbo, also shared her surname with other wardresses working with her. She was a graduate from Potchefstroom University. An Afrikaner from the Transvaal, with at least a bit more knowledge than her two ignorant seniors who felt threatened by her presence. Smith could not hide her jealousy because Erasmus was assigned to the political section. The wardresses have this sort of competition between them, you see. They believed that if you are working with the politicals you are somehow better than the rest. She majored in psychology; she thought she could apply her psychology to us. In the end it did not work, but she tried her level best to make the relationship between political prisoners and herself smooth.

She wanted to see harmony between prisoners and prison staff; unfortunately there is no harmony where apartheid exists. It is not sufficient just to repeat, 'Prisoners are satisfied.' Jimmy Kruger, Minister of Police and Prisons during J. B. Vorster's reign, said in January 1978 to the International Red Cross: 'You are interfering with these prisoners.' He told them that there had never been a complaint from prisoners. Yet at that time most of our political prisoners had been sleeping on the floor for many years. He stated that they had never complained, and who was the International Red Cross to complain? Some people might like to imagine there is peace when there is none, but we do not live in the daydreams of these apartheid gods. We are the people locked up in prison, under these unjust and horrible conditions.

Six

Our biggest complaint remained the food issue. We could not be expected to eat the same trash throughout our prison term. There was this stupid deputy head of Kroonstad Prison, Colonel Steyn. He did not want to see people leading normal lives, even in this rat hole of a prison. Just like the rest he was a racist and a sick racist at that. He wanted to make you feel that you had failed, that you were no longer a human being. That you were going to succumb to everything he told you. He thought he could switch you on and off at will. Being second-in-command of the whole prison, everybody had to dance to his music. We gave him the shock of his life.

One day he came for complaints. We told him we wanted fair treatment, better working conditions and better food. His reply was that he would look into our complaints. Then he said, 'You must bear in mind that the food you are eating is prescribed by a doctor, so really there is nothing to complain about.' He said that in his capacity there really was nothing he could do. There was a diet for blacks and there was nothing wrong with that; a diet for Coloured people, and all that. Those were the rules and regulations and we had to accept them. He admitted though that eating mealies for five years every single day, except on Sunday, was rather too much. He would see what he could do about it, he said, and left.

For some two or three weeks, there was a slight change, an improvement in the meat and stiff pap (porridge) instead of mealies. But then the improvements faded away gradually, as time wore on. We continued with our complaints. Nothing happened. They kept on giving us excuses about prison rules and regulations.

In June 1978 this deputy head of Kroonstad Prison came again for complaints. We again listed them. He answered us in a very unfavourable manner.

'How can you expect us to live on the food we're given?' we complained.

So he said, 'Anyway, you can eat the vegetables; you won't die.'

We demanded: 'What is there to be eaten when the cabbage is

29

rotten, with insects inside; if it is not the cabbage it is carrots, carrots prepared with syrup, with an awful taste! Everything is inedible, né? And you are busy telling us we must eat it, so that we won't die! Then you can keep the stuff, because we won't eat anything, finish and *klaar*. [finished]'

The hunger strike began.

It had never happened in the history of South Africa that women prisoners had been on a hunger strike. At first they thought we were joking. In the beginning there were three of us: Joyce, Esther and myself. By that time Mama Edith was no longer with us in prison; she had been released on appeal. Thandisa Maqungo was a 'freshie', newly arrived on a five-year sentence. We used to sing and most songs were led by Thandisa. She was nineteen when she was sentenced to five years in prison for furthering the aims of a banned organisation, the South African Student Movement, and also for attempting to skip the country to undergo military training. She is a very brave and conscientious comrade. She was locked into the other cells in the same block as Mama Dorothy. Neither of them was involved in the strike because when it started they were not aware of it happening. It was only a day after it had begun that they became aware of it. Lack of proper co-ordination had meant they hadn't joined us.

The first day they brought our breakfast, we looked at the food, just like that, and never touched it. Lunchtime and supper were the same. They didn't take us seriously at first and the second day was the same. Erasmus looked very troubled when she approached us. She tried to reason with us, arguing something like: 'What do you expect to achieve by not eating?' We told her to her face: 'We have nothing to lose if we don't eat. This system is not afraid of scandals; you are used to them. Having killed a person like Steve Biko, then who are we? So we don't think you mind killing us or any other people. We won't stop fighting for our rights. You'd better know that.' We continued the strike for eight days.

The first two days are the hardest. After that you no longer feel hungry. After those first few days I did not feel particularly weak even. From the third day onwards they sent us a doctor. Perhaps they did not want us to die protesting in their prison. They knew that it would cause outrage not only among our people but even in the international community.

The doctor they sent us was full of nonsense. I had to make it clear to the comrades, by saying, 'Comrades, I'm not going to see their doctor. Because I don't need his treatment. I don't want his

30

diet treatment, I'm not ill. What I want is proper food, edible food. I don't see any reason why I should be discriminated against. If you see all those murderers, those criminals, those white criminals who have committed all types of crime, they get better treatment than we do. All I want is good food, just like the white prisoners are getting.'

The doctor went to the other two comrades, and he was full of shit. He told Ausi Joyce that 99 per cent of blacks eat mealies; and Ausi Joyce denounced him to his face. And then when he came to me I gave it straight to him: 'I do not want to see you. I have nothing to do with you. If I am ill I will call you. I have never said I am ill. Oh – go.' I did not give him any opportunity to discuss the situation; it had nothing to do with him, the doctor.

On the eighth day, Brigadier Du Plessis, the one responsible for all political prisoners, showed up. We used to call him MaPine-apple, because Mama Dorothy said Du Plessis' people owned a farm with pineapples some place – she had been a long time in prison, she knew these things. First he called me. He wanted to hear my complaints. I told him I was not willing to take food until they changed the diet, because I was discriminated against. He asked, 'Are you going to tell me that at home you can eat what you are demanding, hae?' 'Yes, definitely. Are your white prisoners, all those hooligans you have here, and these hobos eating that type of food outside? Because some of these are hobos who commit petty crimes, you accommodate them here, you treat them like kings and queens, with all the privileges you can think of. Privileges, just because they are white. And I am denied decent food. I think I am also capable of appreciating good food.'

After that he called Ausi Joyce and Ausi Esther. The two were equally adamant. The three of us told him we were not going to eat, we were not going to succumb to the cruelty of Pretoria. So they told us, 'Okay, you can go back to your section.' And around three o'clock Du Plessis came and told us that yes, they would change the diet. It was our first victory.

That supper was just delicious, properly prepared. We knew we had scored a small victory, so we started to eat again. The following day we got bread. Now that was an achievement – imagine me eating bread during breakfast, man, it was just unbelievable! Lunch was mealie rice with vegetables and soup. On that day, they deliberately prepared the mealie rice in an unpalatable manner, to spite us. But supper was bread – in fact, the type of food Aminah had been getting, but below that standard, the coloured diet standard, to spite us.

The hunger strike lasted from 8 to 16 June. After we had finished the strike, we started planning again. These people did not want to accept that they were defeated. That is why they were preparing the food so badly. We decided to give them another trial. Our strategy went like this: we complained and complained and complained, so that we should have sufficient grounds. And then we acted. We complained from early June until 31 July, challenging them every day about the preparation of the food. On 31 July we went on another hunger strike.

However, the incident that triggered the second action was not only the food issue. I was supposed to get some medicine and injections in the morning. Now in prison they have medical staff, female for female prisoners, male for male prisoners. So Smith came with a man – a warder. She wanted me to undress and let this man inject me. I told her, '*Ai khona* [No, no], you are clowning! Expecting me to undress for this man. Don't you have female medical staff?' She replied, 'They are busy.' I came back with 'It is their work, for them to come and give me the injection. You must not expect me to be given an injection by a man. This is insulting. And secondly you have brought our food late and in this condition.'

The three of us were mad. The second hunger strike started.

That weekend, Sergeant Erasmus, this psychology 'expert', had been off work. She felt terrible when she came back on Monday to find the three of us on hunger strike. She tried to normalise relations by being nice to us, even her manner of talking to us was quite different from that of her colleagues.

We continued with that hunger strike for eleven days. We were moved from the big section we had been staying in, and taken to the section where Mama Dorothy and Thandisa had been; the two of them were moved to our previous section. They came and asked what our complaints were. We told them that the food was not properly prepared, that there were no fluids and all that. They couldn't understand why we were complaining, yet again. We did not want to be given food like pigs. The food had to be edible.

I told them I had another complaint and charged: 'You told me that from October 1977 we could alternate fortnightly with the ironing, but up until now I have been ironing continuously without a break. From today onwards I'm not going to iron any longer. Either give me crocheting work or I won't do any work.' We included my complaint in the strike demands.

There was a period during those eleven days when we were

locked up for a full day. We were expected to stay in our cells and not move about. Du Plessis came several times during that period. He had the gall to tell us we were not people. He'd say, 'Who do you think you are? Do you think you are white?' One of us would retort by saying, 'Is it only white prisoners who can get properly prepared food?' He kept repeating over and over, 'Only whites can get that food – you are not white.' We asked, 'Do you think that eating that type of food will change our colour? There is one thing about colour; it is a biological condition. We don't think that white people are superior in any way to black people. Being black, white or green is not important. We are all human beings.'

We continued with the hunger strike.

Aus Joyce became very ill on the tenth day of the strike. Instead of helping her they threatened to put her in a straitjacket, as if she were mad, and they also threatened to force feed her. They brought the straitjacket. She was weak, but the will power was there. We fought them, the doctor and the wardresses. Later she had nothing left – no reserves, no strength at all. They overpowered her. They dressed her up in the straitjacket and put her on a drip. We thought she was dying.

We discussed our problems at length. What should we do now? They had prepared the food the way we wanted. From the eighth to the eleventh day, the meals looked really attractive and appetising. There seemed to be a real improvement. We concurred and agreed to eat. This was another victory.

After the strike, however, there remained still quite a lot of unresolved issues. There was the problem of parading in the morning. The first bell rang at five o'clock. Every prisoner was expected to wake at five, have a wash, clean the cell well and everything had to be placed in the proper manner in the proper place. The prisoner had to be properly dressed; a red *doek* on, shoes shining, clean apron and stand about a metre from the grille with hands behind the back. When the second bell rang at seven they came to inspect the parade. Now you have to greet them with a smile. If you don't smile, you are not a good prisoner. You are not showing politeness to your apartheid rulers. I was getting really sick of all this.

One day I approached the comrades and said, 'You know, comrades, I think I'm getting sick of all this parading. Tomorrow I'm not going to parade any more. I'll clean my cell, then, with my nightdress on, take a book and start reading. They'll find me reading. No parade for me. I'm sick of it.'

The following day when they came, Erasmus and Bimbo, who shared the same name, they found me sitting at my table, reading or pretending to read. They looked at me once and, as if I wasn't there, Erasmus unlocked my cell and moved on to the next one. Not a word from any one of them. They just moved on.

When the comrades came out of their cells, I was sitting there in my nightdress. 'Yo! Caesarina, you are inviting trouble, you know,' they warned me. I reminded them: 'I told you yesterday that I was not going to parade, and that's that.' Until my release, I never paraded in prison again. That was from mid-September 1978. I couldn't stand some of the rules and regulations the wardresses kept preaching about, and this was one of them. When these so-called rules and regulations were made, I wasn't invited to help set them up, anyway.

Like I said, our main strategy was to nag them with all our complaints and, if nothing was done, then we took action. But with the parade issue there was no time to complain. It would have turned out as a waste of time because they would have repeated the same old song and dance of rules and regulations.

After some time, the comrades supported my boycott. They saw that it was working and they also saw that there was no reason why we should parade for these people. After three days Aus Joyce and Aus Esther were no longer parading. We became more united, stronger. This called for more action. We were going to have to face bigger challenges until victory was assured.

Seven

I started lodging complaints about clothes. I was supported by the other two, Aus Joyce and Aus Esther. I must remind you that Mama Dorothy and Thandi lived in the other section; divide and rule, there must not be unity. They were locked in their section and we were locked in our section, which later was converted into the isolation section.

So, during 1978 we began boycotting prison clothes. We decided not to wear the clothes prescribed for us. I was usually the one who started these protests. Which is why I got the worst treatment from the authorities. I just told comrades, 'You know, I succeeded with the parade thing, and we are no longer parading. Now I do not feel like putting on these shoes. Anyway, I have told these people I wish to wear the same type of clothes as the white prisoners. They say only that there are rules and regulations, these clothes are prescribed for us, we must accept that, finish and *klaar*.' That is what Captain Callitz, the head of the Women's Section of the prison, used to say, and we used to laugh at her for mixing her languages so. I concluded, 'Comrades, you know it seems to me I am not going to put these clothes on.' That was in early October.

And then one day when they came I didn't have the *doek* on, I didn't have the dress on. I had on a petticoat and the vest – anyway I thought it a nice vest, like a T-shirt, a man's vest. And the petticoat almost converted the whole thing into a skirt. Ah, everything was nice. And when they came, the *doek* was sitting there, the apron was sitting there. I didn't put them on. Even the shoes. I informed them that they could take their stuff. They never asked me if I wanted their stuff or not, while with white prisoners they automatically ask, 'Do you want this? Can you come and choose what you want!' Never mind what types of crimes they have committed. And here I am, fighting for my liberation, my rights, and I am deprived of this. I said 'No, I'm sorry, I think this is too much.'

I started the protest; the other comrades hesitated. After some days, Ausi Joyce joined me; much later Ausi Esther joined too.

But now we were clearly divided, as they had intended. Mama Dorothy and Thandisa were living on the other side. The prison staff told them that we were problematic and were into all kinds of trouble. They told them we were going to get everyone in trouble. We used to meet in the exercise yard and we noticed that Mama Dorothy and Thandisa seemed to be nervous in our company, but after some time they joined the boycott.

In mid-October they brought us sandals made with the same material as the shoes. They had been cut with a few holes. They were men's shoes with a few holes; perhaps they wanted to add a touch, a little touch, of feminine sophistication, but it never worked. So we refused to wear them. But Mama Dorothy and Thandisa were wearing them.

'But Caesarina, you were complaining that white prisoners were

35

wearing sandals and you are not.'

'Exactly!' I responded. 'But they are not wearing this nonsense. This is rubbish that you are expecting me to put on. If you are going to give Sonja Swanepoel, the murderess, these sandals, then I will put them on too. But if Sonja is going to wear smart shoes and you expect me to wear these, then you are in for it. I will not put them on!'

And until my release I never put them on, and I made it very clear that I would not put them on. And I think in the process, they began to regard me as a real trouble-maker.

Just at that time I happened to be ill. I had chest problems; I needed to visit the radiologist in town, for an X-ray. They said I would go the following week, although the doctor thought I ought to go immediately. They found themselves in a dilemma, because I was not wearing prison clothes. The clothing boycott was serious, and the doctor was demanding results from the X-ray. I refused to put prison clothes on; yet I had to be taken into town for the X-ray. And I kept hammering them: 'OK, bring me my dress,' and they repeated, 'No, you are not permitted this according to the rules and regulations; you are not supposed to have a dress on and that's finish and *klaar.*' And I shrugged, *'Ai khona.* Then I will have to die in prison and you will have to account for that.'

After about two weeks I saw the doctor again, and I told him, 'You know what? These people do not want me to receive treatment, they just refuse.' Erasmus was standing next to the doctor with a medical staff sister. I added, 'With me, I am ready to go through the door for the X-ray, but they are refusing. You ask her.' And then she answered something like, 'You know, Caesarina does not want to put her clothes on.' 'Doctor, the clothing has nothing to do with going. I do have my own clothes. And they know why I am refusing to wear their clothes. I tell them I will not put their clothes on; I do have my clothes.'

The following day, on a Thursday, they brought my clothes. I ironed them, and after dressing up I looked like a lady. I went to town feeling good. I felt very good that day, going to town, seeing people. A change from seeing prisoners and wardresses in their respective uniforms. Just the pleasure of seeing people in their private clothes relieved my mental state. I was still feeling good when I was taken back to prison after the X-ray.

The prison staff members were livid. Here was a person who always complained; this time she had forced them to bring her clothes. They had even tried tricking me: 'By the way, we have

36

taken your clothes home.' I was outraged. 'Who said so? No! You cannot say you have taken my clothes home, because one, I didn't sign for them, and two, you didn't consult me. If you are expecting me to accept that, then you'll have to give me a dress like Sonja's.'

I was supposed to start writing exams again. They argued that I should not enter the examination room without putting their clothes on. I said, '*Ba hlanya* – you are mad. Who, me? I am going to write the examination, not the clothes. If the clothes can write the examination, okay, you take the clothes and put them in the chair and let them write. Invigilate those things. Caesarina is writing the examination, and that is that. She is not going to put these clothes on.'

So I wrote the examination without putting their uniform on. They tried to turn a blind eye to the whole thing. Eventually I got support. The other political prisoners refused to put the clothes on. Comrades realised this could not be Caesarina's fight alone, and they supported the whole thing. But it started very slowly.

I was confusing the prison, man; they could not understand. Here comes a person, she is no longer parading – and after some few days the other people are not parading. A hunger strike never happened before in Kroonstad – and here are people going in for hunger strikes. We are trying to treat them well but they are never satisfied!

Captain Callitz and this fool Du Plessis began to take the line that: 'You people are never satisfied. When we give you this, you want something more. Every day. I've never heard you saying thank you.' And then we would ask them, 'What is there to thank you for? To thank you for imprisoning us? Then you must be joking.'

I was just insistent. Being cheeky, man, disturbing. I would enjoy it at times. They would tell me it had never happened before in South Africa's prisons. Venter, the head of the prison, once commented that, of the large number of prisoners in Kroonstad Prison there were only three people, three ladies, who were giving them hell. I enjoyed that, that was nice.

They must hate to see political prisoners being brought to that particular prison now. When I left there, in late 1979, the Kroonstad staff were all sick and tired of me.

The clothing boycott continued; it remained an issue until my release. But five years is no child's play.

Eight

Prison life can be dull. Cut off from the outside world, life becomes uninspiring. You see the same faces all the time. At least seeing other faces now and then makes you feel alive. We had tried to find people, through our windows, by straining our necks and standing on our toes. We had turned into being children again. We got excited by trivial things. Seeing new faces now and then excited us. The only new faces were those of short-term prisoners, who looked after our yard.

In front of our cells we had windows. There was a passage, and windows, some six feet or so off the ground. On the other side of the windows, looking through, you could see common-law prisoners. So we used to position the chairs to be able to look through the windows, especially this one very strategic window. It was at the far left of the passage, so you could stand and look down the passage on the right opposite; you could see the prisoners outside.

It was so exciting just to see someone outside our section: 'Come, come Ausi Joyce, here is somebody, she looks like so-and-so of such-and-such place.' And we would try to describe the prisoner concerned. You would feel relieved, pleased to have something to talk about that particular day.

The slightest chance we got to communicate with the common-law prisoners was used to the full. If you want to see prisoners turned into hardened criminals, go to South African prisons. They find ways to outmanoeuvre prison authorities in many ways, and communication is one of them.

We did not get any newspapers but we learned about what was happening outside from the common-law prisoners. They would tell us about current events. These prisoners would stand beneath the window and talk as if they were talking to each other loudly, and we would know that this was a message meant for us. They were so clever, né? Some would stand around and talk, and another two or three would stand at a strategic point, where they could see if the prison authorities were coming. They would relay the message, and in a few minutes would be gone. They would leave us with something to talk about. We would not feel so isolated then.

These prisoners were all women. Some were in jail for *dagga* (marijuana) or murder, pass-law offences, and a lot of other junk. We must not forget the cause of most of these crimes; racial discrimination, oppression and repression. Prison makes visible the evil root of the apartheid system. We used to see a lot of mothers there, some with small kids. It is unbearable to see a baby born and brought up in prison. There was one boy who, at the age of three or four, started smoking, because the whole cell was smoking – the mother was smoking, the other prisoners were smoking. And little kids like this were taught to parade. Just little kids, hands behind their backs, standing the regulation distance from the grille, saying *'Dankie hek* [Thank you, madam].' These kids take it as normal human behaviour, as if there is nothing wrong. They do a lot of damage to our people inside. What is worse is that until I left Kroonstad Prison, not a single white woman had her own child in prison with her. Their kids got cared for outside, because it was thought that their children would be psychologically affected. It is true that prison life destroys children's lives. Their future was being destroyed inside the prison walls.

One day we were peeking through the windows. This Smith, we used to call her Manyonyoba, because she was so good at creeping around. She would turn the keys very quietly, and the next minute you would find her there, in the passage. Unfortunately, that day Esther was standing at the third window on the right-hand side. She heard a little sound – click – you know our ears could work very fast. We snatched the chairs and the blankets, dashing for the other side – and all fell on the floor. Bundle the things together again, scramble to the side – she was opening the outside door to the main passage. Fortunately she turned first to Mama Dorothy's section. We were sedately pursuing our crocheting work by the time she came to us, to tell us it was exercise time. All was calm, nothing looked out of place.

Our main relaxation at that time came from reading. We used to get books such as *The Odessa File, The Day of the Jackal, The Word* by Irvin Wallace, and sometimes historical books like one on Rasputin. Some of these were junk, but we would try to learn what we could from them. For instance, none of us had known there was such a person as Rasputin who actually existed in history. But

39

most of those books had practically nothing to teach us. The staff would just bring the books, perhaps fifty books, and you would choose one. After a time they would collect them and bring in others. But this was looked upon as a privilege. Later we lost even that.

One day the authorities started to block the windows. There had been proper windows; instead they put a four-cornered steel plate, about half a metre high with small holes in it. Those windows were made for storerooms. Really, these people are terrible. I don't have a suitable word for them. They clearly believed they could treat political prisoners like dry goods. And during summer, Kroonstad Prison is so hot – and now we would have to sit in those small, single cells, closed in, without any air coming in.

We complained about the windows for quite a long time. Brigadier Du Plessis, Brigadier Venter, and all their juniors got the complaints from us; but they did absolutely nothing. This continued for a considerable period; so we decided that we had to take action against this type of treatment.

On 2 January 1979 the three of us then staying in the small section decided not to enter our cells: Aus Joyce, Aus Esther and myself. After supper we took our blankets and went out to the courtyard. When Sergeant Erasmus came, we announced: 'Listen, we are not going back to our cells until something is done about the windows. We have been complaining ever since early 1978, and it is now January 1979. It simply means you are not willing to treat us like human beings. We are not going into our cells.' Erasmus said she would speak to the captain. Captain Callitz came. We told her, too: 'Nothing doing, we are not getting into our cells.' They tried to plead with us. We said 'over our dead bodies'.

Both of them left. They came back to inform us that they had phoned Brigadier Venter about the issue, and he had said he would look into the matter the following day, but that now we had to get back into our cells. We questioned them, 'But how can you expect us to live in such a state, in such a terrible place? It's hot, the heat is unbearable, and you have removed proper windows and installed these things. You expect us to be satisfied? We have been complaining and complaining about this. We asked you to put in fans, but you did not do anything about it.' They left us there. Later they came back with three strong men. They said Brigadier Venter said they would have to use force to take us into our cells if we were not willing to go by ourselves. We decided to fight.

Aus Esther's cell was the first from the corner; they tried to take her first. When these men came for her, no, they did not expect it, they were not prepared. We fought back. They surrounded her, the three of them, dragging her. We pulled them off her, hitting them. Eventually Esther was overpowered and dumped in her cell. They pushed her in, locked the grille, and then it was me and Aus Joyce. We fought back again; eventually Joyce, too, was dragged to her cell. I was left alone. Aaiiee, there was serious resistance. I told myself that now I had to just damn well fight. They came, knowing that this one was just mad, mad, mad. I was fighting heavily, punching, hitting them. I ripped one of the warder's shirts, sent the buttons flying bouncing on the floor. I made it a showcase that I landed in my cell with one of his epaulettes.

After all, there is one thing I have learned about this system of the South African government. When you talk soft, they don't listen to you, whatever you say. Until you take action, action in the true sense of the word, where people are fighting physically, not verbally. It is only then that they believe that we mean business. You must hit them hard.

The Afrikaner public servant cannot see any black person, especially a prisoner, oppose any law made by his government. This is because he abides by the rules without questioning them. So they believe that all a prisoner has to do is to abide by the same rules and regulations laid down by the prison heads, irrespective of how stupid they are. With their warped point of view they will not listen to prisoners. There is no democracy whatsoever in the rules and regulations that they are trying to apply in this country. They expect people to succumb to these rules and regulations, to such injustices, to such ill-treatment. I tell you, they are expecting a lot from people. Too much, in fact. Look at a simple case such as this one. We had complained about the windows for almost a year, and this stupid Brigadier Du Plessis was there. We told him that these windows were not suitable for human beings. He agreed that he would look into the matter. But nothing happened; the window situation did not improve until we fought. The following day they unlocked the three cells, but the grille leading to the place where we were supposed to exercise remained locked. And they locked the outside courtyard, the yard to the larger section, so that we could only move in the passage. Usually we would stay in the courtyard after finishing breakfast and do the crocheting work. Now they decided to be funny, because we had refused to re-enter the cells when they failed to meet our demands over the windows.

We decided to go on a boycott again, another hunger strike. And we had other grievances: the meat was no longer properly cooked, and we had been complaining about a few things we needed, like fruits. So for four days we did not eat.

We used to change strategies. We would study the situation, to decide if it was wise to be polite or whether we should be aggressive or just ignore them. In this case we were so polite it was unbelievable. With the result that on the fourth day Brigadier Venter came and asked for complaints. He seemed shocked to find us on hunger strike. He had not expected it to lead to that sort of thing. He thought it was just another prison fight. He never expected organised resistance.

Venter agreed that he would look into the issue of the food being badly prepared and also the issue of the fruits. He claimed there were steps being taken to ensure that all prisoners would receive 'white' diet and it would start at the beginning of April. He claimed he had never instructed anyone to lock the courtyard grille. We pointed out that we had asked Captain Callitz and Sergeant Erasmus why they were not unlocking the courtyard, what this grille business was all about, and that they had said he had given them instructions about this. Venter denied he had ever said this, and he denied it in their presence. He was angry because it seemed certain that his juniors were just giving instructions which he had not said they should give, and that they were creating tension in the prison. Some of the staff members felt they could control us by using the brigadier's name. He said he would look into the matter. The issue of clothing was also raised. He said that he could not change that; it would be handled by his seniors and must be addressed to the politicians.

We got hold of some newspapers from some men who were building a wall to divide us from the common-law prisoners. The Prisons Department reckoned they had problems with the windows; we used to make contact with the common-law prisoners through those windows. So they decided to build a wall between our windows and the yard, I think about a metre from the windows, so that we could not see the other prisoners. They used common-law prisoners to build their wall. But while they were building that wall, as we were grassroots people, we were able to communicate with our brothers.

Besides which, we had cigarettes. In prison, whether you smoke or not, if you have the opportunity of buying anything, buy cigarettes; it is the best bartering commodity. When the International Red Cross came, they gave us cigarettes and chocolates.

We didn't tell them that we did not smoke, we just took them and put them in our rooms. We ate our chocolates and exchanged the cigarettes. There are prisoners who need them. We gave these men cigarettes, they gave us newspapers. Through the windows.

About that time, the brigadier from the headquarters in Pretoria, the head of the prisons, paid us a visit. We lodged all our complaints, food complaints – definitely you just had to complain about the food, that it was not properly prepared. And we wanted fruits which they said were not prescribed in our diet, only prescribed in white prisoners' diets. And we also complained about the clothes. He just said to us: 'You know, maybe with this food thing I can try, but when it comes to clothing there is nothing I can do.' He went on, 'There is something you must know. I am just a civil servant.' We told him straight: 'When you are supposed to check out this problem you are a civil servant. But when you insist that we wear the clothes, you are not a civil servant; you are siding with the oppressor, you are one with them. Why don't you call Le Grange or Kruger to come and make us wear the clothes? If you claim to be a civil servant.' This brigadier could only repeat that it was difficult for him. He would call his seniors.

Later he came with a general. Shame, the poor guy came. By that time we were well equipped with the Information Scandal facts.* He came for our complaints, and we listed our complaints. He made the mistake of claiming: 'This we cannot do, because we are having problems: there is no money to buy clothes.' And then I went for him: 'General, I don't understand when you say you don't have money. You are able to bring fruits to white prisoners. If you are able to bring fruits to white prisoners I think that black prisoners can also get them. About the money issue: it is more serious now that there is this Information Scandal. You are taking all the money to Switzerland, and then you come to tell us that there is no money. Go and tell Vorster that we want our money back from Switzerland.' We sang him a song we had composed after reading about the Information Scandal. *'Si fun imali yethu e*

* In 1978, some Nationalist Party Members of Parliament, including the then Prime Minister, J. B. Vorster, and Connie Mulder, Minister of Information and head of the Transvaal Nationalist Party, who was regarded as the future leader of the Party, were accused of embezzlement of public funds. Both J. B. Vorster and Connie Mulder were forced to resign from Parliament, as well as the Nationalist Party, in disgrace. The scandal involved millions of South African rands.

43

Switzerland [We want our money from Switzerland].' As he left, quite rapidly, we followed him to the door singing at the tops of our voices.

The general was shocked, the brigadier shocked, the captain shocked. Even the sergeant who was looking after us was horrified to find that we were up to date about the Information Scandal. You know, we were talking facts: that Vorster, Rhoodie, Mulder were all involved. We told them we did not expect this type of behaviour from real leaders; real leaders would not steal money, the people's taxes. The general left in a terrible hurry, without any more talk. This created some problems for the sergeant because it was suspected that she had smuggled the papers to us, since she was working with us.

We succeeded in getting the papers smuggled in: the *Daily Mail, Sunday Times* and *Sunday Post.* Reading the good news, such information was very valuable to us. It was something unbelievable. The whole paper was devoted to the scandals, which involved the highest circle of their regime. We got the facts, you know!

'*Jy weet, Aus Joyce die mense ke mashodu* [You know, Aus Joyce, these people are thieves],' I said.

'*Wa bapala wena* [You must be joking]. What good do you expect from them? They are doing worse things than this scandal. If their white community doesn't question anything happening, then forget it!'

'*Dis waar, die anders is net tevrede met* swimming pools *en op die swart man se nek te sit. Ha o bone ba tletse ka ditoronko le dipolicestation, santse ba di aga* to provide employment for them [It's true the others are content with swimming pools and to oppress the black man. They only work in prisons and police stations. They are continuing to build them to provide employment for them].'

To get a piece of a newspaper was like getting gold. So we were very excited about getting these newspapers. We treasured them very much, but even so we could not keep them after we had read them. We had to destroy them. When they came to strip our cells they did not find anything. There was something to discuss, in fact a lot. Imagine! Three whole newspapers! It was great.

The issue of clothing continued, still. When we went to church we went without the so-called overalls, the apron, the *doek.* It must not be forgotten that we had among us an elderly woman, deeply Christian too, who felt a need for due respect. You cannot go to church just in petticoat and vest. But we did not accept that this was what we were doing, as the petticoat resembled a skirt and the vest a T-shirt. And you know Kroonstad is very hot.

During that period we were doing crocheting work during the day, all of us. Aus Esther taught me how to do it, but I was never good at it at all. We had all stopped doing the ironing which was affecting our bodies. There was one wardress named Coetzee who examined the crocheting and took it back to the big offices, right inside the prison where the senior people were. She would come back and tell us that the work was okay, no problems, and she would bring more cotton. We were expected to crochet 20 place mats, and a very big tablecloth. They expected us to spend the whole five years doing that work. It became a problem for some of us. We did not wish to work, not knowing who was going to benefit from it. Moreover, we knew that we were there for no good reason other than that we were black. We had done nothing to warrant being imprisoned. Given all the injustices, I did not see why I should work for them as well. At first I didn't take it seriously, but then things came to a head.

In March 1979, after I had completed 19 square pieces, putting them together, and was busy with the twentieth one to finish a full place mat, Coetzee came to tell me that the work we had been doing was wrong. I said to her, 'Stop clowning, this is serious. I don't see any reason why you should say that, after all this time, after all my effort. After all we have done, you come and tell me that what we have been doing is all wrong – this simply means you are not normal. You examined the stuff, you took it to your seniors to examine it, you always came to us and said everything was okay. All of a sudden you have just decided from nowhere that the work is not right. Okay, I do not have any problem. Also, I do not know for whom I am doing this work. Maybe I am doing it for the most reactionary people . . . so take your work. I am not going to work again in prison.'

I never did work again. From March 1979 until my release, I never again touched their prison work. I am not a prisoner, I am not a slave; I am just on holiday because they have decided to take me away from my public life.

They thought they were going to work me; I made them work thoroughly instead. Everyone who thought of me during my imprisonment ended up shivering, because they thought I was a very difficult person to control. Which of course I was; you cannot just make life easy for them. I told myself and I told them that I was not in that prison to work for them. They took on that employment, which was to look after me. So they worked for me. And I made sure that when they got their salaries they felt that they had really earned that money, in a very difficult manner.

We were joined in prison by Mancane, that is, Elizabeth Nhlapo, who was sentenced to five years for recruiting for MK, and by Mama Mita Magano, also sentenced to five years for helping people to leave the country. Sibongile Mthembu who was in for two years, plus four years suspended, convicted of sedition, also arrived. And we saw Feziwe Bokolani at Kroonstad, I think, for five minutes. They brought her in, she came, we greeted her – and she was taken away immediately. I think they imagined we would influence her to be radical; they think there are some people who are a bit better than others, even in prison. So we only saw each other in Pretoria for a couple of hours, much later.

During that period in Kroonstad resistance was growing. There were the complaints about food, the clothing boycott, and complaints about wardresses with negative attitudes toward us; there was serious resistance to all apartheid laws, giving the regime real problems. So the staff made an attempt to see if the prisoners could be divided. During our hunger strike we stated that we were not only fighting for ourselves, but for every single prisoner who was convicted. We made it a policy to fight for equal treatment. This was our battle. But when Elizabeth Nhlapo and Mama Mita Magano were brought to Kroonstad Prison the authorities decided they were going to give these two different food from us, yet again.

We fought that from the outset. We made it very clear to them that what they were doing to these people would lead to another hunger strike. We were not going to accept having different types of treatment: eating, sharing the same table, with the one eating porridge and the other eating mealie rice. It was humiliating. Moreover, what we were fighting for in general was for everybody's benefit, not just for the people who had taken part in the boycott. We should always remember that the apartheid regime grows fat by dividing and ruling. We made it explicitly clear to them that if they did not stop what they were doing to our comrades, we were going to boycott their stuff. And knowing us by then, they knew we were not playing.

They had the gall to inform us that, after all, it was only we who had fought for the food, these new people had not been there before – so why should they benefit from our actions? Which was complete nonsense. The freedom we want, the democracy we want in our country is not for a few people, but for everybody, irrespective of colour or class. It is for all of us.

That shocks them, you know. When they see us fighting for others, as in this case where newly convicted prisoners were differently treated, they are taken by surprise. They themselves really believe, and they try to poison our people's minds into believing as well, that what you fight for must be yours only, never mind about the next person. And we completely defeated that poison in prison. We are here as sisters, fighting for one thing; we are united by oppression, by apartheid, united by the imperialists, united by the exploiters. And when we stand so united, we can break these exploiters. Totally.

I appreciate what the comrades stood for: it took courage. The people said 'no'. During our time we made life really miserable for the system. They had been under the illusion that they would just break us, turn us into *ja-baas* (yes-boss), divide us, break our spirits, shatter our unity. We made it clear they would never succeed in chaining our spirits. They had the idea that putting us in prison would solve the problem, keep us quiet; it surprised them that even in prison we said 'no' to the apartheid regime, we said 'no' to the oppressors, we said 'no' to the exploiters. We demanded equal treatment, resisted all their discriminatory laws.

And there is a lot of discrimination in prison; there is a lot of apartheid. We had a great deal of work to do, and there remains much to be done to teach these people that we are not going to succumb. If a person does not know his or her standpoint, that person can be suppressed, silenced. But if you know where you stand, if you know that the people support you, you will keep on resisting wherever you are; whether in Leeukop, in Pretoria Central, in Kroonstad, in Pollsmoor, on Robben Island. You say 'no' to the apartheid regime.

When the International Red Cross came for the second time, in 1978, we told them that we would like to see Jimmy Kruger himself. We had quite a lot of complaints which the prison staff kept saying they could not handle, because they were not politicians, they were civil servants. Jimmy Kruger was a politician, but Jimmy Kruger refused to come. We had first made this request in January; in August they told us that Jimmy said no, he was not willing to see us. Because we were trouble, we were causing problems in prison, he was not prepared to see such people.

47

Nine

During that period before the Easter hunger strike our complaints multiplied. They changed the diet of the other prisoners, but we went to them and pointed out: 'You said you were going to give us the same diet as white prisoners, all of us. You did not, and until such time as you do that, we will fight on. We want to get the same treatment.' We were more united and the comrades started chanting:

> We want equal treatment
> We want equal treatment
> with the white prisoners
> with the white prisoners
> Food, clothing, everything

They did not meet our demands. On 8 April 1979 we went on strike. It was to be our longest strike, 17 days. It was a Sunday when we sent the food back and went to church.

When I started to serve my sentence in Kroonstad they had a white chaplain. His name was Pretorius. He was there every Sunday, conducting the church service, choosing chapters in the bible that he used to try to brainwash the black prisoners with. He was always trying to make us feel guilty by preaching how bad we were and how we could not escape the raging fires of hell if we did not obey our jailers and the laws of the country because the rulers were chosen by God, and stuff like that. We got very sick of him and demanded his immediate removal and another chaplain in his place.

They brought us an old black man. To my great disappointment, this black chaplain, who belonged to the Dutch Reformed Church somewhere in the black township serving Kroonstad, read out a special chapter. He must have been briefed about what chapter to read and preach about to us. It was where St Paul says the people must obey the rulers of their country because they were chosen by

God. Agh, you know, we were mad. Here is this person who actually does not understand our plight inside prison; but that particular day he preached, saying we must obey. During his service everybody sat up. They told us which hymn to sing. Instead we sang:

> South Africa Ikhaya lam
> engili thandayo
> Sizo kuwu lwela umhlaba wethu
> size sikhulu leke
> [South Africa is my home
> which I love. We will fight for our land
> until we are free.]

Poor soul, he was frightened. During the last prayer he couldn't utter the words properly, he stumbled on, quavered that God must help us to change our hearts which had gone to something like hell. He used the Setswana words, '*Modimo a re thuse re buse dipelo tsa rona tse ilong mafiso* [May God help us, may our hearts be humbled which are in hell],' telling us that we must come back, listen to our rulers, listen to the people who were appointed by God to be the rulers of our country.

As for me, from that day onwards I refused to go to church in prison. When they came to say it was church time, I would tell them: 'You go and tell that priest that he must pray to all the apartheid gods that they must change their hearts so that all people can live properly together in this country. When he does that I will go to church. As it is, he thinks my heart is in hell.'

The hunger strike continued. On Tuesday Colonel Steyn came and asked for complaints. He had informed us some time before that we could eat the mealies and that if we didn't want to we could eat rotten cabbage, we wouldn't die. We had made a decision that we would not make any more complaints to this character. When he came we simply did not say a thing to him. We just looked at him and ignored him. He went away, furious. We told Sergeant Erasmus that we would like to see Brigadier Venter. She asked us, 'How can you say you want to see Brigadier Venter when Colonel Steyn was here?' We retorted, 'We don't want to speak to stupid characters, you know. Because we will end up fighting. We would like to see the brigadier.'

It seems he got the message. Though he didn't turn up that very day, he did come the following day, Wednesday. We were busy doing exercises in the big yard. He didn't say anything to us, but walked straight through our section of the cells. By that time we were fuming over the way they were treating us, our request, our strike. The plates with the food were strewn on the floor and the trolley was upside down; when we went to the exercise yard we had pushed the trolley to the wall and it fell; the plates came off and the food was all a mess on the floor. Brigadier Venter had come specifically to tell the staff that he did not wish to see us or speak to us, and he went away. So on the Thursday before Good Friday, the seven of us, Aus Joyce, Aus Esther, Mama Mita, Mama Dorothy, Thandisa, Mancane and myself, trooped to the exercise yard. We foresaw trouble. Some of our comrades were new; they didn't know how far they could go, how strong they could be, how to resist some of these things. Some of us were used to these people, you know; we had track records. We knew how to handle them.

Venter refused to see us. So when we were supposed to return, we said we would not go into the cells before seeing him. They came and told us to return to the cells. We said, 'No, we like to socialise. We don't see ourselves going into the cells; it's a long weekend, and this problem, the hunger strike, is not yet solved.' So they resorted to violence. Instead of calling Venter, they came with seven men. We fought back, hitting them with benches, but we were eventually overpowered. Each warder matched a prisoner, but they went as a group for each of us at a time. I was bundled into the wrong cell, Aus Joyce was bundled into the wrong cell, so was Aus Esther. The rest went into their own cells.

On the morning of Good Friday they brought us food and we refused to take it. We demanded that we go back to our own cells and they replied, 'We will unlock the cells as soon as we can get in touch with the brigadier.' They came back an hour later. They unlocked the cells. As we were moving out they were saying something about locking us in for the whole day, and I grabbed the keys from the wardress's hand with the intention of opening the other cells where our comrades were still locked in. She had come with three men, heavily built – you know those Boer boys who are built like rugby players. Perhaps they were. They came after me but were blocked by the others and tried to throw us into the cells. We challenged them: 'Come, just try. We are not getting into those cells.' Realising that we were fighting, they went for reinforcements. When they came back they were nine men and four wardresses. They came for us with batons, the men leading, and we retreated into the passage.

Now the passage was normally kept locked beyond our cells, to form a dead end. Mama Dorothy's cell was right at the back. Thandisa's cell was the second down the corridor; Mancane's by the corner. The three of us moved right to the back, up by Mama Dorothy's cell. So that when they come for us they couldn't reach us. They had to pass Mama Mita's cell first, so Mama Mita took hot water from the basin and poured it over them, and they went back. We were using all sorts of weapons: plates, bottles, spoons, steel mugs, soap – Mama Mita, Thandisa, Mancane, Mama Dorothy armed us with anything they had, and we would throw it. We made a kind of jellied soap from the washing soap, né? Not powdered soap but Sunlight. If we had a small piece left we would put it into a tin and pour on water to form this jelly soap. We took that and poured it on the floor, so that when they came for us they slipped. And we had Vim that we used as tear gas.

Ausi Joyce is a short woman, tiny, small-built. She was jumping up and down and shrieking, 'Voice of Reason or War! Voice of Reason or War! Voice of Reason or War!' Glaring at this tall, huge man. There were screams as we were trying to confuse the enemy. Throwing benches, chairs, plates, food – anything we could think of. And this Vim, floating in the air, turning into a blinding fog; and this soap, water – soap, when they came for us slipping, falling; the Vim doing its work, the soap doing its work, the plates doing their work. When they approached us they would just go down, into the pools of soapy water, on the floor.

They came at us with dustbin lids and batons. They eventually overpowered us after some time, by adopting the very same strategy we had initiated. They used Vim. Vim in the face, it went into our eyes and we were blinded. And they came for us. We were taken to our cells.

Months later, we got a charge: refusing to get into our cells, né?

During this time of fighting, please remember, we had already been six days on hunger strike. The hunger strike had started on Sunday 8 April; the first fight was on the Thursday, and the second, the Voice of Reason or War, on Good Friday. By then we all had empty stomachs. Full people, people who had eaten a delicious breakfast, who had filled up on healthy food for the whole week, came to fight women they thought must be weak from not eating. But perhaps they did not know that you can get really angry when you are hungry.

Once back in our cells, we made a resolution that we would not bath, we would only wash in our rooms, our single cells. No one was to take a bath, no one was to exercise, we wouldn't take their food, we wouldn't speak to them. The only thing we accepted from them was the medicine. During that Good Friday when we fought with the warders and wardresses some of us were injured. I had very bad backaches. At one stage I felt that maybe my spinal cord was out of joint. We agreed that those who were receiving medicine should take it; although it was quite dangerous to take medicine on an empty stomach, we had no option.

There was a certain medical staff sister, one with stupid attitudes. That day, when she was rubbing my back, she asked, 'But Caesarina, why are you people so difficult?' And I asked her in return, 'What do you mean?' She replied, 'You ask for food, the food is okay, everything has improved. But you are creating more problems, particularly you. Just have a look now, you have a backache.'

By that time we had reached a stage where they surely knew our feelings. I told her: 'Listen here, it is none of your business why I have a backache. Your duty is to care for my health not to look at what I am against. You know that you people are treating us like pigs; you are treating us like moving machines, and do not regard us as human beings. And you are expecting us to say, okay *baas, dankie baas,* we succumb. That's stupid.'

We had many visits from prison staff members, asking for complaints. Now we took a resolution that we were not going to speak to them: they knew our position. They would come and we would ignore them. We called it 'dis', for 'disregard' – you 'dis', you give them 'dis'. That one weapon completely frustrated them; they became flustered. They did not know how to handle that.

We were drinking lukewarm water. It makes a person feel strong, despite the lack of food. They left us locked in our cells. Maybe one of us would stand at the grille, talking; another might sit at the table, or lie on the bed – it depended upon the individual.

Throughout the hunger strike period we would sing to keep our morale high. Our favourite songs were:

> *Nawo amabungu eAngola*
> *Ayoza nazo, kwedini*
> [There are the warriors in Angola
> They will come back armed].

52

Another one:

> Siph' amandla Nkosi okunge sabi
> Siph' amandla Nkosi okuba nqoba
> [Give us strength Lord to be fearless
> Give us strength Lord to conquer them].

And another:

> Bam' uMahlangu
> Dubula, bulala nge aka
> [They have murdered Mahlangu
> Shoot, kill with AK].

It was a terribly trying period, striving to prove our strength. We felt like asking Medimo (God) to give us strength, because amongst us we had real Christians such as Mama Dorothy. We had to build each other's fighting spirit. It is not a bed of roses this road to freedom.

The hunger strike continued until 25 April, for 17 days. That final night, in the small hours of the morning, I think around three or four, comrade Elizabeth Nhlapo woke us. She was ill, physically ill. She had had a kidney operation some time ago, before her conviction, I think when she was on trial, and she was still weak. We were fast asleep, all of us, each in her cell, when Elizabeth started calling Thandisa, whose cell was opposite hers, asking for water.

Thandisa could not give her water as she was not in the cell with her. We were all locked up separately. We could not help her. And Elizabeth could not even reach the bell in her cell, she was too weak. The only thing we could do was to ring our bells – each of us had a bell in the room. We rang: they came. We said: 'Look at that comrade, go and attend to that comrade who is ill.' They went to her, they attended to her – and then they said they were going to put her into a straitjacket because she refused to eat.

Hai, we foresaw some difficulties. Some of us were still strong. But the minute they were able to force one of us to eat – putting Elizabeth in a straitjacket would mean that – everything would flop. It was the first hunger strike for Mama Dorothy, Mama Mita, Mancane and Thandisa. Three of them were elderly, too. We could not be sure that their health would hold up.

To be honest, I felt 'Aaiiee, I would be better dead'; but the comrades talked some sense into me. There is no point in trying to be a martyr. We now decided that because of these problems we would end the strike. And it was not a total defeat. We had made significant gains. We now got peanut butter, sometimes; jam and margarine regularly, alternating with cereal. So we called it off.

Despite having had to end the strike, that resistance helped the new prisoners, the new comrades recently convicted. They gained courage from seeing women who resisted. When these new comrades arrived, they found us not parading; immediately they joined us – and now none of us would parade. That parading was disgusting, humiliating – how could they expect you to be polite to them while they continued to control your life, to control your everything? These new comrades were fortunate: on their arrival they discovered that '*A luta continua!*'

After we ended the hunger strike, we terminated all the boycotts. We decided to take baths, exercise, that type of thing. But they did not unlock us. They announced that we had to stay in our single cells; they took us one by one to exercise. From that Thursday before Easter when we fought them, we stayed locked in our cells all the time – no more moving about in the passage.

And they restricted our exercise time, too. Before, we used to get 90 minutes exercise a day: 45 minutes in the morning and 45 in the afternoon. After we were segregated we got only 30 minutes exercise a day. They argued that they did not have the time to take each prisoner out separately for the full 90 minutes allotted.

Which meant that we would spend 23 hours and 30 minutes out of 24 locked in our cells. Spending 23 hours 30 minutes every day in a cell is mentally destroying. I started talking to myself, laughing to myself, at times I was turning paranoid.

At one stage they decided to take us out two by two; two for bath, two for exercise. Then they would lock the outside door where the two were doing exercise. The rest would stay locked up in our cells. We grew eager just to see each other's faces. It was now quite some time since we had seen each other. Although we were talking to each other through the grilles, we could not see each other's faces.

We demanded an explanation. We were told that we would be segregated indefinitely. Until our attitude, our behaviour, stopped. Until we improved ourselves. Putting their clothes on, no longer complaining – because we were complaining continuously, even though we were no longer on strike. They were trying to tame us, to show us that if we did not do what the prison authorities wanted us to do we would remain locked up.

They stopped all our studies, they took away all the library books. We no longer got visits. We no longer got letters or toiletries. Everything which was classified a privilege was taken away from us. That was their strategy for breaking us. They never learn, these people; it is going to take time to teach them that material things cannot break the spirits of dedicated people.

So after these things were taken away, Sergeant Erasmus came and said that I was supposed to sign a certain card.

'What for?'

'To record you are no longer Group C or D.'

'Well then, if I am no longer in any group, C or D or whatever, why must I sign anything?'

'To prove you are aware of that.'

I told her straight: 'With me it does not make any difference. Whether I am group Z or whether I am group nothing, it is just the same. I am not here for groups, but for my liberation. For equal treatment. And I am not going to give in because you have removed the groups. If I wanted to remain with a group I could have got everything at home without ever knowing that there was any group thing. I wouldn't have known it in this prison. So you can just take your damn groups. I am not here for privileges. If you feel that treating people like human beings is a privilege, then you can stuff it.'

And she went away.

That was in June.

Then, one day I was taken out for exercise together with Thandisa. They did it deliberately. That day they had so many warders out, I think there were about eight warders and three wardresses, outside in the exercise yard. And they took the two of us for exercise. It was a trap.

They used to enjoy it, you know. We were stubborn, and they knew that we were stubborn; and they beat us, bundled us, put us back into our cells and locked us up. Then we would start to shout at them, telling them such a lot of things, the type of cowards they were.

That day we were not long out and they announced, 'Time up.' We revolted, we said no. We had not been out for 15 minutes and they were telling us time was up. By that time they were standing over us, man, you know; warders and wardresses armed with batons. They think that beating people, killing people, can solve their problems. But that is no solution to our problems, a fact which they refuse to acknowledge. Their threats of violence only make our people more resolute. They think that if they show us an iron hand we will break. Unfortunately for them they will never succeed. That time we were taken to our cells by force. Fighting back again. Later we got charged for that, too.

After the hunger strike, we saw they were busy in the isolation section; and we realised that now, something was going to happen. These people intended dividing us physically where they could not break the unity of our spirits. It worried us.

On 4 June 1979, a woman came – she was a colonel by that time, Colonel Van Zyl. She asked for complaints. She started with Aus Esther, who gave her the cold shoulder. My cell was the next one; she wanted me to be on parade, fully dressed. I said, 'One, it is not my other dresses which are speaking, it is not my standing up which is going to lodge complaints. And two, don't expect miracles. How can you expect me to respect you when you are treating me like this? How can you expect me to show any respect to your apartheid regime?'

She sniffed and said that she was not willing to listen to my complaints because I was too arrogant. I replied, 'Okay, you can just go to the nearest hell, because I won't beg you.'

She went to the next cell. Aus Joyce told her shit too. And Thandisa followed suit. The colonel tried to be polite to Mama Dorothy because she had been so long in prison, they all knew her. They spoke for some minutes. She went around asking for our complaints, then informing us that we were arrogant.

We grew angry. Eventually it ended with everybody shouting, telling her anything, you know. Which of course was quite good, in that it let her know that even if she had become a senior among the apartheid people she was nothing to us, just another apartheid goddess. To hell with their attitude towards us.

In June 1979 they charged us. I was given a charge sheet with 16 counts, Thandisa was given a charge sheet with 16 counts, Aus Esther was given 15 counts, Aus Joyce 15 counts, while Mama Mita got 12. Every count could result in 30 days' spare diet. What is most interesting about these charges is that 12 of them were about refusing to put on clothes: because every day when they came in the morning they asked, 'Why didn't you put your clothes on?' And they wanted you to reply. But we gave them 'dis'; we ignored them, said nothing. They wrote down that we were not commenting. Every day for 12 days they did that, and they charged us for each day.

It was this fool Du Plessis who started this charging nonsense. He threatened us with it. He would say: 'Do you think you are white?' It was his favourite catch phrase. They had so many possible charges. If they were to charge me from when the whole thing started in October 1978, if they were going to continue charging us for every offence, imagine it! Charging us for an incident a day for five years, sentencing us to spare diet for five years. That would certainly be a record.

So they came up with 12 charges for refusing to put on uniform, and four charges for refusing to go into our cells. They held a trial. On these charges they tried us in their internal court. We were entitled to legal representation, all that nonsense. They found a magistrate from the Prisons Department, Kroonstad Prison, a total fool; he made such stupid mistakes. And the prosecutor arrived, also from the Prisons Department. You could not expect anything except a verdict of guilty.

But we wanted to speak to our lawyers, to discuss it with them. For quite a long time they had refused us permission to see our lawyers. There was this prison instruction that we were not permitted to write anything to our lawyers, to say anything to our lawyers unless we were only talking about the appeal. Once your appeal is over, forget about your lawyer. At least now, even though we would face only this internal court, we would be able to speak to a lawyer about our conditions in prison.

But then they declared that the case could not continue unless I put my overalls on; they claimed we were naked wearing petticoats and vests. And we realised that if we did not compromise in this by putting the overalls on, it would be self-destructive, counter-productive. Tactics say you look for loopholes, you compromise if it will give you an advantage. So we put the overalls on, and we went to our lawyers.

We thought that by seeing our legal representatives, we would be able to tell them, and they would be able to tell the world, that we were suffering, that the whole of the South African prison system is rotten.

My case started in July. They asked us to plead and we pleaded not guilty. I was represented by a Mr Makombe, a lawyer from Mamelodi.

The day I put my overalls on I was compromising. I could always change my tactics and go naked. But, after all, here was an attorney I could not disappoint. In the morning I went to court in the overalls, but not wearing the *doek*. The court commenced,

57

proceeded, adjourned for lunch. After lunch I went back. But before the court resumed the magistrate said he could not continue with the case because I did not have a prisoner's uniform on.

Before my attorney could open his mouth I blew up. 'What? Having a uniform on – do you think I beg you? Just now, hardly a minute ago as I entered this damn room, I saw a white prisoner, convicted of any type of crime you can think of, wearing smart clothes. And you are expecting me to put on a *doek*? Why don't you tell the white prisoners to wear *doeks*? What is it that you are trying to hide on my head – or are you expecting me to hide my head from something? We are all prisoners; we must get equal treatment. I am not going to put a *doek* on.'

I was really mad. I felt like attacking that magistrate physically. In prison you reach a stage where you are scraped raw, where your emotions ride on your back.

The attorney, my attorney, turned to me. 'Okay. What you must do is go and put the *doek* on.'

'No, I am not going to put it on.'

'I am asking you, please go and put it on.'

Yerrah! When I went out of that room, *ke ne ke hlanya ke ho kwata* [I was raving mad with anger]. I was screaming down the whole passage, telling them a lot of shift, né? When I went into the section where Aus Esther was busy doing exercises, she said, '*Plau*, Kona, what's wrong now?'

I told her. 'These bastards are telling me to go and put a *doek* on.'

She was clear: '*Ba hlanya; ke eng ba o gapeletsa?* [They are mad; why are they forcing you?]'

And then the others were hanging about like monkeys peeping through the windows. Aus Joyce shouted 'What is happening?'

'They have said she must put a *doek* on!'

So we all started up abusing them – 'These apartheid gods think they will oppress people forever' and all that. I went to the cupboard. I put on that *doek*, put it on to prove I was angry but that I respect this attorney. I re-entered the courtroom and sat down, boiling over.

But before the court could proceed, my attorney announced that he had realised that the magistrate was biased. According to the rules of legal procedure a magistrate must listen to the case before he makes up his mind on the outcome. If the magistrate was going to instruct the accused to obey the complainant on the very issue the case was supposed to decide, it was obvious the magistrate had already taken sides. So my attorney had to politely request that the

Prisons' Department find an unbiased magistrate.

The court adjourned. That particular magistrate was thrown out of the case. It was an achievement, seeing a white magistrate being chased away from court by prisoners and their attorney.

After about three weeks the headquarters people sent another magistrate, this time from prison headquarters. He tried not to force issues. I didn't wear the *doek*, I wanted to see how he would react. I didn't wear the *doek*, but the case continued calmly. They had a group of wardresses saying that they had given me instructions for a very long time; saying that I refused to put the clothes on, that I had been instructed to enter the cell and had refused.

The case dragged on until September. I was sentenced to 60 days' spare diet.

Man, 60 days is not child's play. The spare diet we were supposed to receive went like this. You served it in periods of 30 days, probably to keep you from starving to death. If you got 60 days, you served 30 days, then had an interval of 14 days, then started with the second 30 days. In the 30-day periods you got (with slight differences from one prison to another) what we call 'spare' for the first 12 days out of the 30. Porridge, without salt or anything at all, certainly not sugar; or stiff pap, *phuthu*, without salt or anything. (At Kroonstad we got *phuthu*.) And soup – your lunch – brown powdered stuff, a spoonful of which is tipped into a steel mug full of water. That is all. Supper is *phuthu*, without anything. For 12 days. You get nothing except that. After 12 days you get half-meal, half of everything you would normally get, what the other prisoners are eating. If they get a slice of bread, you get half a slice. If they are drinking a full mug of tea, you drink half a mug. Half ration of everything. The next six days you get full diet, the same as the other prisoners are getting. The remaining six days it is back to spare; stiff pap, soup, stiff pap. And they ration the whole thing. Most of the time you are simply hungry. At the same time I think it makes a person strong; it teaches you to deal with real hardship.

During the interval, the two-week interval between spare diets, you eat full meals. Then you start again.

This is what I got for 60 days.

The process did not end there. We wrote letters to Le Grange, who took over from Jimmy Kruger as Minister for Prisons, Police and Justice, that he should come to see us. We had complained to all his staff members, brigadiers, commissioners of prisons, generals, you name it; they all said they were not politicians, that we had to speak to the politicians. So we wrote letters to Le Grange, each of us writing a letter in her own wording to avoid pinpointing one single person as the leader.

He came some time in October. It was on a Thursday in late October 1979. He came with an army of his prison staff, from wardresses to the commissioner. We were all together; I was collected fresh from the isolation section to be with the others. We told him all our complaints. And we wanted a reply then and there. But he only said, 'We are not going to push you.'

Now this has to be the most stupid man I have ever seen. People came with genuine complaints, but he was not willing to solve these problems, when it was his people, taking his orders, who caused these problems. He said he would consider the issue of clothing. And I replied that I didn't see him considering the issue of clothing; he must just give us a reply there and then. His white prisoners were leading a soft life, we also wanted to live a soft life. He went on that yes, well, we were making life very difficult for his staff members, there was a lot of confrontation.

Aus Joyce answered: 'Confrontation is on both sides; I cannot confront a person if the other is not confronting me. So you should educate your staff members, because your staff members have very undermining attitudes.'

He left without giving us any proper answers concerning the food issue, the clothing issue, behaviour of staff members, and the problem of spending 23 hours and 30 minutes in the cells, going out for 30 minutes and coming back again.

Ten

The farce in the internal courts went on; meanwhile the struggle continued in our daily lives as well.

During this time there was the wardress called Mbomvana. You know, I hated her like hell. I don't even remember her real surname. Because she was so red, we just called her Mbomvana, which means red. She had this attitude, that she would deal with s brutally. here was one thing about us: if a person decided to be difficult, to show an iron hand, we would retaliate the same way. I think she made us more stubborn, and for sure we were already stubborn.

Before the internal trials, on 8 June, in the morning, they brought breakfast. She brought us porridge which was not properly prepared, stiff and raw; I think they cooked it for three minutes and served it up. And they came in a big crowd. We were wondering, uh, what is happening? Because here are so many of these people, men and women, just to bring the porridge. They just stood around in the passage. It was clearly not all right.

We called to them; 'This porridge is not okay.' Mbomvana said she had prepared the porridge that morning and she was satisfied that it was okay. We told her, 'You are talking nonsense, man. How can you say this porridge is okay? Have you eaten it?' She replied that she was not a prisoner, she was not going to eat prisoners' food.

So I spelt it out: 'Then you are cooking shit and coming to tell us it is prisoners' food. You are not a prisoner. So you are doing all this deliberately.' We picked up the quarrel; everybody was after her. Suddenly they changed their line, 'Thandisa must take her stuff, because she is going.' We demanded, 'Where to?' even before Thandisa could ask 'Where?', because we felt she was just part of us. We asked them, 'Where is she going?'

Her cell was unlocked. They got two men, huge men, tall and healthy, who just grabbed her, beating her on the way. I saw them: ta ta ta! Banging on her throat. They dragged her to the isolation section, and dumped her there.

I was the next victim. I was not expecting this, standing in my cell and cursing them for their treatment of Thandisa. Not knowing that they were coming for me. And they just bundled me, too, took me to the cells. On the way I was telling them a lot of things. That they were afraid of our brothers on the borders, let them go to Angola, SWAPO would shoot them to pieces, the bloody fucking cowards, they were just ill-treating women, knowing that we did not have weapons, anything; I'd just smash them to pieces anyway – after liberation. I would just show them. They started beating me. They were hitting me with a baton, seriously hitting, yo! I was dragged into a cell and dropped.

My old cell was stripped. Most of my things were taken away. They only brought the clothes. That was in the morning. They brought lunch. After lunch they left the cells and went away.

That afternoon this Mbomvana came again, in the company of

61

one we called Yita. I don't remember her surname, either. She unlocked the cell. The men were standing in the courtyard. She said to me I could go and have my bath. She took Thandisa for her exercise and locked her into the small courtyard.

I was hardly three minutes in the bath when she came and told me, 'Come, your time is up.' I objected. *'Au, o a hlanya*; you are insane. How can you say time is up, I have not even washed my face? How long do you provide for bathtime?' And she said 'Fifteen minutes.' Then I asked her, 'Do you know the meaning of 15 minutes? Because I have not even started to wash my face and you are telling me that my time is up.' By that time I was sitting in the bath, naked. She locked the grille, went to call the men. And they came.

You know, Mbomvana, this stupid wardress, had a boyfriend, one of the warders at Kroonstad. And her boyfriend, whose name was Roet, came with another man called Else. They swaggered into the bathroom, lugged me out of the bath, naked, water running off me. And they started smashing into me with batons. All over my body. They pulled me to my cell, one on each side, hammering me with their batons. They dumped me there like a sack of potatoes.

That day I was raving mad. In my anger, I swore that I would never forgive these people. Actually I made it very clear to them that after takeover, if I happen to be alive, they are the people I am going to kill. I am going to hunt for them, to make sure. After liberation, if I happen to see it. No, I won't die before killing you. It cannot be otherwise.

Of course, it was not solely her fault, this Mbomvana; brought up with the idea that you are a superior being, that you have to be on top of the black woman or man's head, that a black woman or man cannot say anything, she or he must take what you give because you are the *baas*. These characters are brought up like that; but still she's one of those I can't forgive.

The following day Brigadier Venter came. In fact, immediately after the beating I rang the bell and said I wanted to see the doctor. Because I must record proof, to lay a charge against them. They told me the doctor was not there. And I reminded them that the doctor himself had said to us that if we wanted him to see us he was willing to come at any time. So I didn't see any reason why they said the doctor was not there.

The next day, before the doctor came, I saw Brigadier Venter and made the complaint about the beating. He defended the assault: according to him, I had refused to go into the cell, and he had given instructions that if anyone refused to go into her cell she had to be taken by force. I said: 'I never refused to go into the cell. This woman has a bad attitude towards us, particularly towards me. She thinks she is in a position to discipline us. I had not been long in the bath and yet she came to say time was up. This was done deliberately. And she decided to call her boyfriend and a friend to beat me up.' And I informed Venter that I wanted to lay a charge against them. Then I saw the doctor, who gave me a thorough examination. He wrote down everything. I was really ill.

I want to make it clear that this Mbomvana was a real sadist. We – Thandisa and I – decided to plot against this Mbomvana. Because, with all our sufferings in prison, this sadist managed to make life even more miserable than it normally was. But also because by now we were despairing of ever getting our situation improved unless we could get into court *outside* the prison. At that time we were in the isolation section, just the two of us. And I said to Thandisa, *'Mchana, wa tseba Mbomvana wa tella* [Comrade, you know Mbomvana is full of nonsense]. We must just show her.' I wanted to handle her alone, but Thandisa refused. 'No man, this is not the best way. We must just *donner* her [beat her up] together.'

Before they took all the study materials away, Thandisa had gone into her isolation cell with a box of mathematical instruments. We shared the instruments out between us, those with long, sharp needles. I smuggled one into my cell; Thandisa hid the other.

The following morning (it was on a Sunday) Mbomvana unlocked the two of us; bath time. We decided we would ambush her, take her off her guard. We were going to be so meek. When she unlocked us in the morning we would just smile at her, all sugar. And she would be under the impression that we were now subdued, defeated.

She unlocked me, greeted me. I said, 'How's it?' and she got excited – you know, she actually got excited, she could not believe it. That here was someone greeting her so nicely, this one who was her enemy, perhaps this one was now broken. And she got the same treatment from Thandisa.

And she made the most stupid and dangerous blunder of her career – she unlocked the two of us at the same moment. She was confused; she had expected the usual big problems from us, she thought we were the two most difficult amongst the comrades. When suddenly she found only sweetness and light. And she went blind to reality.

63

The two of us moved politely to our different bathrooms. We had agreed that when she came to lock us up I would pretend I was still in the bath, né? so that she had to pass my bathroom and go to Thandisa's. And she fell into our trap, blind.

So when she came in, still bemused by her petty victory that we had greeted her properly and a bit smiling that morning, she did just what we planned – went straight to Thandisa to lock her up. And then I jumped out of my bath, immediately, without even drying myself, ducked into the nightdress and ran after her.

And I said, 'Eh, Mbomvana, why are you treating us like this?' She turned, 'Like what?'

I demanded: 'Aren't we supposed to get exercise?' and then, before she could answer, I slapped her. Thandisa went for her. We took the instruments; we started stabbing her.

A wardress, Hekal, was standing there. They had by that time closed the grille, the outside grille to the big yard. We gave Hekal a few claps and she just fled, she was absolutely terrified. Man, she made it clear that she did not want to involve herself in Mbomvana's problem.

And we went for Mbomvana. We stabbed her several times with those mathematical instruments. We had made up our minds that this person was not going to treat us like this; we wanted to kill her, there and then. Let us kill her and they can hang us. Because we have had enough of her. We assaulted her for a long time, stabbing her in the face, on the head, on the body, all over. She was bleeding on to the passage floor. After we had satisfied ourselves we went back to our cells.

There was confusion, a lot of confusion, in the passage. Hekal was whistling frantically. Mbomvana staggered down the passage, bleeding, into the other section. The other comrades were hanging on the windows, staring. We passed all the instruments to a comrade outside of isolation. There were two big drains; that comrade threw the instruments into the drains. We wiped up the blood on the floor, on our hands, removed any potential evidence we could see. Everything had disappeared – except for the blood on Mbomvana's body; she was covered in it.

Don't forget that all this was on a Sunday. As Mbomvana stumbled out, common-law prisoners stood there gaping at her. She used to harass everybody, irrespective of kind. During lunchtime we could hear the common-law prisoners ululating, cheering, singing, praising the beating. The other comrades – Aus Joyce, Mama Dorothy, Mama Mita, Aus Esther – all rejoiced. It was a nice fight, with a person who was giving us all a heavy time. She had got it at last, from those who were not afraid of her. The small kids had decided to solve her.

Some 20 to 25 minutes after her ignominious departure they brought their men to bring us back under control. They were surprised: each was already in her cell, very cool, sleeping in her bed as if untroubled by bad dreams. And they were well and truly frustrated, believe you me; they were looking for an excuse to hurt. They could only lock us up and go away again.

The following day, on the Monday, the staff came in as usual for complaints. We gave them the usual list. But later that week they brought the South African Police into the section. The police announced they wanted to take our statements. We replied, 'Nothing doing. We are not going to make any statements. We will talk to our lawyer.' So they went away.

They removed me from the isolation section to the big section – which was also isolation, as all of us were segregated. The day I was taken there they got a shock. They thought I was going to say no. Instead of sending a wardress to tell me that I was supposed to go to the other section, they brought men to escort me. Hai, this time I was determined to act the lady. To be honest I can be a very decent lady if you are a lady to me; but if you decide to be difficult, I am also willing to be quite difficult. I refuse to be a lady when other people are not ladies. It is too expensive.

But I sailed gracefully into that other section. When I reached the cell where I was supposed to stay, Aus Joyce addressed me, 'You know Kona, I think you are very intelligent. You know these people. I was listening to them but I didn't know how to pass on the message to you. Because they were planning how they were going to beat you up.' It was clear that the boyfriend was really furious because Mbomvana had been seriously wounded. He wanted to retaliate; but I did not give him the opportunity.

When the South African Police came some time later I was in the big section, together with Mama Mita and Aus Joyce. Ausi Esther and Thandisa were in the other isolation section, serving their sentence, spare diet punishment.

Whenever a case in prison involves blood it is always referred to the South African Police (SAP). This means the case is no longer in the hands of the Prisons' Department. When you are found guilty your prison sentence is increased. Depending on its seriousness, the case is heard at either the Regional Court, or the Supreme Court if it involves murder. In Mbomvana's case it was to be the

Regional Court, which is why the SAP came to us.

I was in the exercise yard when they came, talking to Thandisa through the windows of the isolation section. Mbomvana approached:

'These police want to speak to you.'

'What for?' I enquired.

'They want your fingerprints.'

'*Uthini Kona? Uthi bafuna ntoni?* [What is it Kona? What do they want?]' Thandisa wanted to know.

'*Amafinger prints* [They want fingerprints],' I replied.

'*Ungavumi ga!* [Don't let them do this shit!]' she said.

'*Asoze ndi vume* [I won't let them].' Turning to Mbomvana, 'My fingerprints! What for? I don't want this.'

I had hardly finished talking when they were on top of me. They didn't say anything but started to beat me. They took the fingerprints by force. At that time we did not know it was illegal to refuse.

And then those policemen started to beat me up. Eh, they went for me. Thandisa was telling them nonsense through the window; I was telling them nonsense, too. I told them they were afraid of our brothers on the borders who were giving them hell. They should go to Angola where our brothers would blow them to pieces. And that our brothers would be coming back, and they would never forget what they saw then. You know, some of those policemen looked really frightened – we were telling them about what was actually happening, not forgetting the fact that many of them had joined the police force because they were afraid of being drafted into the army. Here were people talking about reality: that they were in fact losing in Angola; and here they were beating up women.

That afternoon, after they finished with me, they went to Thandisa and beat her up too, forcing her to give them fingerprints.

We said we wanted to see Captain Callitz. She came. I lodged a complaint that I had been beaten up by the SAP, that I wanted to lay a charge against them. Her only reply was that she was not in a position to say anything, as the SAP were handling that assault case. All she could do was to call the man in charge of the SAP.

So a certain lieutenant came, that very same afternoon. And he informed us that it was illegal for suspects to refuse to give fingerprints. So that if we continued with laying a charge against them, he was going to lay a charge against us likewise. All I said was: 'Listen, I have been beaten up; I have evidence. You can see my body is full of bruises. Whether or not you are going to lay a charge against me for refusing to take fingerprints, I am going to lay a charge of assault.'

He went away.

He came back twice, trying to convince us, trying to threaten us with charges. And I just maintained I would go ahead with it.

One day when we were still in the bigger section, Mbomvana took me out for exercise. She was accompanied by Hekal and one warder we used to call Dikaledi. Outside there was a bench which we used to sit on. I took the bench, put it opposite Aus Joyce's cell and spoke to Aus Joyce through the windows. Thandisa was taking a bath and watching me take exercise; Aus Esther was also in her cell. And while I was sitting there Mbomvana marched over. 'You are not supposed to be sitting there.'

'Is this not a prisoners' bench?'

'But you are supposed to be doing exercise.'

'This is not your bench. If I decide to sit down it has nothing to do with you.'

She repeated, 'No, you must get off this bench.' By that time she was standing next to me. She grabbed the bench and tried to pull it out from under me. I knew I was about to fall; I decided to take her with me. I clapped her. We started fighting. Dikaledi and Hekal were there and began to assist her, hitting me with batons. My comrades could only watch us through the windows. Thandisa began screaming at them, telling them to leave me alone.

So they left me in the yard, shouting, to go to lock Thandisa up again. But when they came to lock her up, she demanded to know why they were fighting with me. They told her it was none of her business. At that point, Thandisa said, she had a wet towel in her hand. She slapped Mbomvana with the towel, spat in her face, and slapped her some more with the towel. So they started fighting with Thandisa, too. It was some time before she was overpowered.

You know, this is a real comrade. A comrade who will defend you at whatever risk to herself.

I was still in the big yard. Aaiiee, I was angry, steaming, hatred flowering. They called some men to take me back to my cell. I was seized by the arms and thrown in the cell.

And then came 31 July. Three of them were bringing us lunch. Because Dikaledi had been involved in beating me up, when I fought Mbomvana over the bench, I was furious with him. I pointed a finger at him: 'Why did you beat me up that day?' He did not answer me, but Mbomvana did. I slapped her and we started fighting. All three were armed with batons.

I had never been beaten up like that before. They laid into me. Honestly, né, they took their time and beat me thoroughly. I was pushed into a corner of the cell. Mbomvana and Else both held my hands so I could not fight back. And all of them hit me wherever he or she could. And they continued hitting me for a long time.

No one could help me. I looked for weapons, there was nothing. But I couldn't stop, you know – I did all I could, using a lot of vulgar words, speaking angry, telling them all sorts of things. After some time they decided to shift, to leave off. They left my hands loose. When they had first come into my cell, they had put my lunch on top of the cupboard. I grabbed the plate full of food and threw it into Mbomvana's face. The fight resumed. Aaiiee, the fight resumed. They came back into my cell and they went to town with me. That time, to be honest, I learned what helplessness meant. I couldn't do anything. I was beaten. Every part of my body was screaming.

When they left, I just dropped on top of my bed and cried. Everything was painful; but what made me cry most of all was that I knew that if I had been able to kill Mbomvana, it would have been better for me. At least I would have known that I had killed this one pig who had made my life so miserable.

About 15 or 20 minutes after they had locked my cell, Mama Mita and Aus Joyce began to call to me. They were so worried, asking me how I felt, how it was. Because even the wall tiles were broken, even the toilet basin was cracked, the cell was in chaos. How did I feel? 'Eh eh eh eh, Aus Joyce. Really comrade, *kajeno ba mpetditse ha ke batle go bua maaka* [Today I was seriously beaten, I don't want to lie].' My eyes were swollen, my nose was big and I had cuts and bruises everywhere.

That lunchtime, Du Plessis, the stupid brigadier, came. He said that because I was a trouble-maker, they now had to put a chute on the door. The room normally had a grille and a sliding wooden door which the prisoner could open for air or close for privacy. They were proposing to lock the wooden door as well as the grille (which was normally locked) and feed me only through a chute. You can imagine what this man was trying to do. There would be no air; he wanted me to suffocate in that room.

My comrades revolted. Aus Joyce and Mama Mita stated simply, 'Nothing doing. You are not going to do that.'

Immediately after he left they came to put the chute in. Then they locked up that section.

Aus Joyce and Mama Mita insisted on seeing Brigadier Venter. The following day the brigadier came in the morning. When he arrived he announced that he would like to see us all together, not one by one. I think he thought it would teach the others a lesson to see how I looked. Because I was a wreck: swollen eyes, bruises, cuts.

Aus Esther, Aus Joyce, Mama Mita, Thandisa, we were so united. They were clear. 'No, we are not going to permit this. No one is going to lock up our comrade like that. This man is not prepared to see peace here. Eventually this comrade will end up going mad if she is locked up like that.'

Brigadier Venter reversed Du Plessis' decision, on condition that these other comrades talk to me, that I stop fighting. So they did not proceed with the chute. If they had continued with that I do not think I would have lasted for long.

After all this the two of us, Thandisa and I, were called into Captain Callitz's office. There we found the SAP and the magistrate and the prosecutor. They announced that we were charged with assaulting Mbomvana, once for the time we had stabbed her, once for the time she provoked me in the exercise yard.

The case would have to be taken to an outside court.

Now this, as I said, had been one of our main aims. If we could, we wanted to create an opportunity to let the outside world know that we were getting this type of treatment inside, that we were discriminated against, and so on. The outside world seemed completely ignorant of what was going on within South Africa's prisons, particularly with regard to the women political prisoners. People just assumed that we were inside, and that it ended there. We had known that if we injured a wardress seriously enough, enough to add time on to our sentence, their rules and regulations called for a proper trial in a proper outside court. With the attendant publicity.

And we succeeded. This case was taken out. During the court case we were represented by a certain lawyer from Port Elizabeth called Fitchard. I gave him all the details, the complaints I had tried to lodge, the charges I wanted to lay against the SAP for beating me up, against Roet and Else for beating me up in the bath, against Else, Dikaledi and Mbomvana for beating me when they brought my lunch. I had the evidence, the doctor had given me a written report to say that I had been wounded all over my body.

We went to the outside court, as I said, for assaulting

Mbomvana. As we approached the court buildings we became intoxicated by the sight of so many different faces. We were singing. And you know these stupid Boers? They gave us a guard of honour. People watching grew puzzled, because while prisoners frequently come to court they don't often get that kind of escort. When we realised they were trying to chase people away we started chanting. People turned to see what was happening. We got out of the van and gave the people's salute. The people responded. It was exhilarating. After so many years, here were the people, our people. A lot of prison warders and wardresses were trying to hurry us into the courtroom. We hung back, took our time. When we reached the court they chased out some of the people attending other cases, trying to make it a special case. This only attracted more attention.

The first day, Mbomvana came to state her evidence, that we had assaulted her blah, blah, blah. Hekal also gave evidence. And they called this Dikaledi to give evidence too.

But when we were asked to submit our evidence, we let loose. This was our opportunity; we had to tell the outside world what was happening in prison. They had begun to separate us, taking Mama Dorothy, Mamncane, and Sibongile Nthembu to Potchefstroom. We elaborated on the issues, that we were discriminated against, ill-treated and that the white prisoners . . . ah, we just went home about the white prisoners. We emphasised the racial discrimination in prison. We also detailed the people's resistance.

We made it very clear, then, to the court that these Boers were dodging the issues. That we had legitimate grievances, we had been complaining, and they would say they were civil servants whenever it suited them. That we had asked to see the relevant minister, Jimmy Kruger, in charge of prison services, but that he had made it very clear he was not willing to see us. That these people were consciously oppressing and ill-treating us and generally making life miserable for the political prisoners.

It all came out in the press. Even the fact that we had asked to see Jimmy Kruger and he had refused.

The judge found us guilty, which hardly surprised us as we had undoubtedly stabbed the wardress. But he must have felt a little sympathy, or perhaps the publicity we received forced him to behave reasonably.

Thandisa and I both received 60 days on the first charge, for assaulting Mbomvana with mathematical instruments. The judge acquitted me on the second charge, for fighting with Mbomvana in the courtyard. He found that she had provoked the quarrel. But Thandisa received 30 days on the second charge. These sentences were added on to the end of our five years.

When we went back to prison, the others were almost through with their punishement for having refused to enter their cells, put on their clothes, etc. I still faced punishment for these offences, in addition to the punishment for attacking Mbomvana. It was a bit tough but I said 'a luta' and continued to press my own charges.

The attorney, this Fitchard from Port Elizabeth, had also taken on my three cases for assault by the SAP and the Prisons Department. The charges were: (1) assault in the bath; (2) assault on 31 July in my cell; (3) assault by the SAP when they beat me over the fingerprints issue. But before long he told me to get another attorney, that he himself could not handle the matter. I accepted this, only to find that he, Fitchard, had made a total mess of the matter. I received a lot of letters from him. Then another attorney from Mamelodi came, saying he had been requested by Fitchard to take statements from me. I saw him once and gave him my statements. Next thing I heard that Fitchard had left the country and was working for the Boers.

Sometime later, when I was in Klerksdorp Prison, a warrant officer called me; I was wanted on the phone. Receiving a phone call in prison? It was another attorney I had never heard of, a Chetty from Durban. He told me that he would come to see me the following day, but I never heard from him again. The case just shifted from one lawyer to another.

A full two years after the assault, I received a letter from the Attorney General of the Cape of Good Hope – who knows how he got involved in this – telling me that one of the cases had been quashed, but that I had to pay all the court fees. I knew nothing about that, since the case had never reached court at all. Another letter came, regarding the SAP case, claiming that there was insufficient information for the matter to be pursued; besides it was too late to lay charges. I ask you! I gave the damn lawyers all the information immediately, in August 1979. How can they tell me two years later that the information received was too late? It looked crooked to me. Reading between the lines you could see that the lawyers were deliberately sabotaging these cases. I began to wonder who these lawyers were really working for: for the people or . . .?

I wrote to Priscilla Jana, one of the political lawyers fighting the regime. We discussed all my cases at length. She was fed up with the way they had been mismanaged. But she felt there was nothing we could do, that we should drop the charges.

I got those 60 days' spare diet from the internal trial. According to prison rules and regulations you cannot appeal against the sentence. So I just served it. But I want to make it clear that this matter is not yet finished.

I began my first 30 days' spare diet. By that time Aus Joyce had finished her punishment and had returned to the big section. I was left alone. Aus Joyce argued that she would like to remain in the isolation section until my sentence was through, but they said no.

They locked me up in the isolation section alone. They wanted to spite me, to discipline me. And then, when I was in that isolation cell, they painted the window panes with white paint, so I could not even look out, could not see anyone. Comrades in the exercise yard outside attempted several times to scratch the paint, so that I could see just a small piece of the yard and see their faces. The whole cell was dark, and I had to burn the electric lights 24 hours a day if I wanted to see. The whole section was painted white, the windows were white, the walls were white. They cut me off from humanity. I was in prison within a prison.

Nothing. Nobody. I could hear comrades speaking in the yard. I would talk to them, but I could not see them. When they tried to scratch off the paint, the following day the warders would paint it again. It was a heart-rending effort with no success for long.

I could only talk to my comrades during exercise period. We tried screaming to each other, across the sections. 'What did you eat today?' 'How did it taste?' Trying to remind myself that at least people were eating. They would call me, asking how I felt; the comrades were very supportive. And everybody was furious. They felt frustrated, but they did not know what to do.

There was nothing, nothing. No bible. No reading material at all. I was there on my own. Twenty-three hours 30 minutes went by like this. I was taken for a bath. After the bath, exercise. Back in the cell. For the next 23 hours 30 minutes, speaking to myself, singing, laughing, thinking, growing paranoid, hallucinating. You think of all things.

I got depressed. The anger, the hatred was building.

It affected my mind. At about eight o'clock in the evening I would hear footsteps, and think, 'These people are coming to kill me.' It worked into my mind.

There was this fan. They had a very big fan installed after we complained about the blocked windows. Immediately after supper they would switch the fan on. It made a noise like a generator, that drrrrrrrrrrr; and I was alone in there, about to run mad. Listening to the noise. Thinking that maybe they were deliberately putting on the noise like that; that they had locked me in here alone, so that they could come and finish me off.

This can destroy you.

Nobody could say anything to me. I would just explode. The wardresses were the only people I was allowed to speak to, and that was only when they came to torment me. Everything they said to me was wrong. I attacked them verbally; each time they replied I just became more angry.

But this anger helped me to be strong. I used to ask myself a simple question: here are people trying to frustrate me, trying to break me. But am I not fortunate, compared with Solomon Mahlangu?* Just that one question I used to ask myself, and I gained courage and strength.

Solly came from my area, Mamelodi. I had seen him around; he used to sell peanuts on the trains when he was a kid, a typical township kid. And he joined the people's army, Umkhonto We Sizwe, after training he went back to South Africa to fight the racist regime. This he did out of his love for freedom, his love for justice and peace. The South Africans captured him and they executed him. Even then I was able to tell comrades, *'Re lehlohonol o re sa phela, re sa bona tseo ba re etsang*. [We are lucky to be alive, we see all their viciousness]. I think we are fortunate.' Whenever I thought of Solly I said '*aluta continua*'. Whatever they were doing to me.

My comrades in prison tried hard to help me. Just talking to me, yelling to me; it is important to hear a person's voice, to know this person is sharing your problems, your plight. It counts. Scratching the paint was a struggle. Even if it marked only a temporary victory, it was such a joy to see even a part of a face through that scratch.

Comrades did try to get extra food to me; they struggled to break my spare diet. On a Sunday they had this delicious steak. All four of my comrades went all out to give me a large donation. The first person to be taken out for exercise at the same time as me was Aus Joyce. She was in the big courtyard, I was in the small courtyard.

*An *Umkhonto We Sizwe* guerrilla who fought and killed two policemen, according to his charge sheet. He was sentenced to death and was later hanged in Pretoria.

But she is so short, you know. She tried to throw the meat, which was wrapped in paper, over the wall into my courtyard. And the meat landed on the roof. It made a crashing noise. Everybody's heart was painful. Because you know at least comrades tried; she wanted to prove she was eager. If they could have left the meat for some time, left it to dry, given it to a taller person. She tried so hard, and then it only landed on the roof. But the attempt proved their solidarity. It means so much, in such a situation. Where you are really united the enemy cannot enter.

While Aus Joyce was serving her sentence, I was moved to the isolation section again. Actually, I had told them I wanted to stay with Aus Joyce in isolation; in any case I would be going there soon enough as my case was about to finish. I planned to stay with Aus Joyce and assist her, as we were afraid that since Aus Esther and Thandisa were now out of that section, Aus Joyce would suffer. We might not be able to smuggle food to her.

I pointed out to them that staying alone in that place hurts you mentally, it can seriously affect you. We soon found out how right I was; at that time, they agreed, and I went there, staying in the cell near Aus Joyce.

Most of the time I managed to smuggle the type of food I was eating to Joyce. In fact it was quite easy. But there was this once. She had been given her breakfast, *phuthu* without anything, and it was still hot. I wanted to pass this food to her which we had been given the previous day: meat and vegetables – for once even the cabbage was well prepared. We were in adjoining bathrooms, locked in, and there was a locked door between us. Our method was to use plastics – sanitary towel plastics were very valuable commodities – which we used to cover the smuggled items. Wash the plastic thoroughly, put the food inside, press the stuff flat and slip it under the door. That day I was very keen Joyce should have the meat. I shoved. The plastic tore. There was a big piece of meat jammed under the door. I struggled, I urged it to move. We heard them unlock the door and enter the courtyard. Jesus, were we shivering! We did not want them to discover the smuggling, for they would definitely take me straight back to the other section. And Joyce would suffer. If they unlocked the door they could not miss seeing that meat. And the meat did not move.

Fortunately they went to the bigger section first. By the time they got to us, we had just pushed it all through. Man, were we relieved. They came and unlocked – I was supposed to be taking a bath; I had barely splashed water on myself.

'Are you through?'

To be honest I had been long in that bathroom. Of course, I said: 'Yes, I think I'm through.' They had their suspicions, but they couldn't find anything out of place. I washed in my room, in the basin.

We used to smuggle a lot of things. It kept our morale high, daily defeating their rules and regulations.

They thought that, by taking the other comrades away from us, they would prove that we were the bad ones; they could force us to repent. But we had nothing of which to repent. We knew what we wanted; what we wanted was simple justice. Nothing more, nothing less. That was our strength. We also knew our people, our comrades, were with us, and that gave us courage.

I spent two-and-a-half months there, alone. From August until the end of October.

That segregation was the most destructive part of the sentence. If I had had to stay there until November I would have gone raving mad. I was on the brink of it. Fortunately I was transferred to Pretoria.

Whenever I think of it, that hatred starts up again. I am trying to outgrow it. But when I think of that particular period – they ill-treated me always in prison, but those months I will never forget – I think I will not ever forgive those people. Of course anything is possible, but I don't think I will change in this respect.

At times I think I am tough. They did not break me then, either.

Eleven

They transferred me to Pretoria at the end of October. I reached Pretoria around five in the evening and was taken straight to the new prison, still called Pretoria Central Prison. It was smart, beautifully built compared to the old Pretoria prison, compared to Kroonstad. You know, when I got to that new cell I thought I was staying in a posh hotel, just because of the windows. Those windows!

The Kroonstad staff said they were sick and tired of me. They could not control me. They were all reluctant to work in that section; they said I was creating more problems than any other person in the whole of that big prison. Perhaps they thought that by taking me to another prison, breaking me away from my comrades, they would force me to succumb. At least they themselves would no longer have to deal with the problem. I would become someone else's headache.

And the staff members at Pretoria had that iron-handed attitude; they were determined to discipline me where Kroonstad staff failed. Immediately I arrived there, that same day, they started to act as if they were tough.

I just looked at them andd thought: they don't know me. They will see me in my true colours.

When I came in there was no toilet paper in the room. I asked quite politely, 'Wardress, would you give me some toilet paper because I do not see any toilet paper in this room.'

She answered with something like, *'Man kan jy nie sien dat ek besig is nie?* [Man, can't you see that I'm busy?]'

I exclaimed, 'Why, listen to me. I am talking to you in English! I expect you to address me in the same language.'

This was Bothma, who knew me from my detention in 1976. She snapped back: *'Hoekom probeer jy om snaaks te wees? Kan jy nie die taal praat nie?* [Why are you trying to be funny? Can't you speak the language?]'

I shrugged. 'So what if I know the language, I am allowed to speak any language I like. And at the moment I prefer to address you in English.'

She was shocked. Or perhaps she was not really so shocked, because she must have been warned beforehand what she would get. They usually send a report with the prisoner, that she is one two three. The Pretoria staff presumed that by being a bit harsh they would make me collapse, just end up so meek. Many of the staff there knew me from when I had been in Pretoria before; they thought they would sit on top of my head.

Aaiiee, but I think they regretted it when I returned to Pretoria. I was no longer awaiting trial or a detainee but a convicted prisoner; this time with full knowledge of my rights, this time with full knowledge of my strength. And approaching them in a politically mature way.

Immediately I arrived at that prison the prison staff started to serve my sentence with me. Each prison had its part to play. It is not nice to serve a sentence alone, the warders must not be allowed to think you are unearned wages. I used to tell them that they must not think they would enjoy those fat cheques as easily as all that. After all, we were all in this prison together. Uh huh.

So the following day I launched some complaints about the food. It was Bothma again. She replied, 'You know I have heard all about your nonsense; don't think you are going to bring that nonsense here.'

'What nonsense are you talking about?'

'I have heard about it; this is Pretoria, not Kroonstad.'

I demanded, 'What is the difference between Pretoria and Kroonstad? There is no difference. There is one thing about me you've got to understand. I want you to know my policy. I am going to walk 50 kilometres; and I am expecting you prison staff to walk the other 50 kilometres. We are going to make it a hundred. I am not going to walk 100 kilometres like that alone. That is my policy. If you are for sport I am also for sport, né? If you are quiet I am also quiet, and if you are a darling I am also a darling.'

And I quoted the prison regulations, that the prison warder or wardress must be an example to the prisoner. So however they behaved, they would be setting an example for me.

'If you are going to greet me I will greet you; and I expect you, being an example, to greet me first. If you don't greet me I am just going to look at you like that, because I don't get anything out of greeting you. In fact I'd be doing you a favour.'

When they first locked me into my cell at Pretoria, I started to sing. Being in favour of revolutionary song, I was giving voice to a favourite of that period, *'Ayoza nazo'*. And you know, I heard somebody responding. At that time, we had received false information that Elizabeth Nhlapo had been transferred to Pretoria. I hoped she might hear me, but the prison was quite big and my cell was on the third floor of their isolation section. I kept on singing, very loudly, and somebody was responding – yo, I got excited. After some time I heard somebody shouting *'Amandla!* [Power!]' I yelled back: *'Nga wethu!* [Is ours!]'

Man, this was nice. I didn't know how to handle everything, locked in a new cell, uncertain where to stand, what direction to shout in, and not knowing who such a person could be. There was definitely no way, then, that I could see anyone, this unknown comrade. But somebody was responding to my music. It was weeks before I could identify this comrade who welcomed me in the name of the people to Pretoria Prison.

In Pretoria, unlike Kroonstad, they used both black and white wardresses to look after political prisoners. There was one fool called Sergeant Kekana from Atteridgeville who was a total puppet. This Kekana had an Afrikaner mentality, although she was black. To the whites she was a *ja-baas*. But to those under her she acted like a bully. She made a great number of enemies, amongst prisoners, amongst her colleagues, both black and white. Nobody trusted her. She was regarded as a sell-out. Even staff members would say, 'You know this character, we don't know what to do.' Her seniors knew all about her. We have such cases where a black person forgets she is staying in the township, that she is suffering together with the very same people she is helping the oppressor to oppress. Such a person forgets that after helping the oppressor she has to go back to the township. That Kekana treated all of us terribly badly.

And there was one wardress called Rita, also from Atteridgeville; that one tried to be polite to us. There was one again, from Mamelodi, called Maponya. She knew me from home, she knew my people. She was friendly, too, but one always wondered whether one could trust these characters, even the polite ones. Kekana usually worked in the political section, with yet another white wardress called Erasmus – there are so many of them, these Erasmuses, in South Africa. Just like the Bothas, another common Afrikaner name. At least this Erasmus would talk to us as though we were human beings – which is quite unusual under such circumstances. Her parents owned a farm around Soutpansberg, which I gathered was quite a large farm, with cows and horses and other livestock. Many Nationalist Party bigshots visited her parents' farm and they would sit around and talk. Erasmus told me she heard these people talk about taking over Mozambique, Zimbabwe, then still called Rhodesia, Angola, and the other countries surrounding South Africa. They were saying that that was what was promised to them by P. W. Botha because of the loyalty of his Afrikaner backers. Of course I was not then in touch with what was happening outside the prison walls.

There were some strange aspects to my conversations with Erasmus. Once we were chatting and she mentioned that they were going out to shoot. I asked her what they were shooting. She replied that they were learning how to shoot straight. The target was a board with a black man painted on it, with various parts of the body circled. They would shoot at the board, and the person who hit the indicated parts was congratulated. They are instilling the idea that they have to know how to kill black people.

I questioned her. 'Tell me, if they are teaching you how to shoot, who are you going you shoot? Are you going to kill black people?'

Her reply was, 'If it is necessary, yes.'

Here was an honest Afrikaner woman, who told me without any hesitation that she would kill if necessary. I realised what troubles lay ahead. Although I was in prison, I knew that people were dying in the streets, black people. The monster urged by hatred was running loose in southern Africa. The cry for justice that landed me inside these prisons was the same one I was to face when I came out. What kind of human beings were these?

Kekana and Erasmus were responsible for giving me exercise, baths and all the other things I had to have; I got no privileges. When I arrived at Pretoria I moved straight to segregation. That first two weeks in Pretoria, I was in the interval, the regulation 14-day interval between my sentence of two 30 days' spare diet. After two weeks I was due to resume the punishment.

But when I arrived there the staff decided to spite me. They gave me too little food. Bothma did this deliberately. She thought that she could solve her problem that way. She claimed that I was a *'harde gat'* (tough nut), so she would be the same. I complained. I told her, 'This is not my ration. This is not the amount of food I am supposed to get.'

She said that she would weigh my food. And then she gave me two spoonfuls of each.

And I sighed, 'Eh heh, I don't have any problems with the food issue. You can keep your food, and I'll do without it.' Remember, that Monday I was fresh from the 30 days' punishment spare diet, and I was expected to start a new 30 days in two weeks.

So immediately, I started a hunger strike at Pretoria, alone. And that continued for a full seven days. They could not believe it. When the doctor came, he asked me why I was not eating. I told him: 'Your people are not willing to give me food. And since they are not willing, I won't take it. Either they make up their minds that they are going to give me food, or they starve me. That's that. I am not going to beg for food. I am not going to beg them.'

They tried to be stubborn. On the fourth day of my hunger strike Brigadier Du Plessis arrived in the company of Van Zyl, who had now been promoted to the rank of Brigadier. I decided that these people were too stupid for my liking; I was not going to continue to speak to fools. I just kept quiet. I gave them 'dis'.

They asked, 'Any complaints?'

I looked at them and then went back to sleep on my bed.

They turned and left.

On the sixth day Brigadier Van Zyl, who was then responsible for Pretoria section, came to see me. He asked for complaints; I gave them. He said that he would attend to some of these problems, then added: 'But you know, Caesarina, you are a real problem. I've read about you. You gave people problems at Kroonstad, and now you think you are going to give us problems.'

And I laid it out for him, clear. 'Listen, if your people are not willing to give me food, no problems; you can keep it. I have nothing to lose, you know, but my own chains. I am the one who is suffering, I am the one who is oppressed. I am the one who must fight for my rights, no one else is going to fight for me. I cannot expect miracles, I cannot expect freedom to fall from heaven. Definitely not.'

Food happens to be part and parcel of a person's life. While in prison, food assumes major proportions; there is so little to life there, anyhow. Locked up, getting 30 minutes' exercise, with nothing else to do; not receiving proper food affects you. If the food is bad or too little, it is frustrating, painful. It's a form of torture. All you are supposed to get in that place is the bare minimum you need; if you receive less than that minimum you get angry. Even the preparation becomes a critical issue – imagine being given a whole plate of shit. I just told them that this was not what I was going to take, and that was that, finish and *klaar*.

The following day there was a great improvement in the food. In the afternoon they decided that, after all, they would give me proper food and full rations. The business of giving me too little food was scrapped.

Indeed, because of the hunger strike, they could not proceed with the new spare diet sentence immediately. According to the doctor's recommendation, I had to stay another week on full diet to make it a full 14 days. Some of those fools did want to make me start the 30 days' spare immediately. But looking at my health the doctor said no.

Usually the medical staff in prison are all the same. They come, they take your pulse, they say, 'Okay, she is fit for punishment, she can start eating pap.' This doctor could be like that, too. But perhaps they thought that if they started the spare diet punishment then I would stop eating altogether.

After an extra week of normal rations I resumed the spare diet punishment. The spare diet at Pretoria differed greatly from

Kroonstad in one respect: at Kroonstad we ate *phuthu* in the morning and *phuthu* for supper, whereas at Pretoria we got porridge in the morning and porridge for supper. Not so good, né? The soup was identical. And everything else was the same, too – there was nothing else at all.

Fortunately, during the seven days of full meals after my hunger strike, I managed to hoard some sugar from my rations, with the result that for the first 12 days I did not feel it so much; I would put some sugar in my porridge, eat something sweet.

Then one Sunday in November, while I was still on punishment, a wardress came with my food. And I objected. 'No, this is too little.' By that time I had finished with the spare and was eating half ration; but that plate contained not even half, it was a quarter. So I protested, 'No, *ai khona*. This is not the half-ration I am supposed to get.' She picked it up and took the food away. When she came back she brought two warrant officers. You know, I was fuming in the cell.

And they started, 'Caesarina, we have something to tell you.' Me, I was only concentrating on the food issue. 'What is it?' 'We have bad news for you. Your father is late; he was buried yesterday.'

I could not believe it. Man, my father was buried yesterday. Anyway, I retorted, 'Aaiiee, what can I do? Okay, I've heard that. There is nothing I can do. Let's come back to the issue of the food.'

The three of them were honestly horrified. They expected me to turn hysterical, certainly to forget my complaints. They stared at me. They had thought that maybe this would crush me. That at least, seeing I had lost a parent, for once I would stop my campaign. I told them, nothing doing. We would continue with the food issue.

They went away again and returned with my proper ration, my half-ration, a reasonable half-ration. What I knew I was supposed to get.

These apartheid gods, they can be inhuman, cruel. When my father died they knew about it, but they kept quiet. Then they came to tell me, in the midst of a quarrel, that the old man was late. They refused to permit my people to come to tell me; they refused to allow my late father to come to visit me; they used the information as a knife in my heart, and expected me to weaken, to turn hysterical, to crack into pieces.

They allowed me a visit of ten minutes from my Mum after that. The last time I had been permitted to see my mother was in

February 1978 at Kroonstad. We had family to talk about, my son, my late father, so much. Visits in prison bring on homesickness; they leave you feeling the pain. That you have lost so much being locked up in there.

After my father had been buried they continued with the total segregation. For the two years and six months that I was kept in segregation I received no letters. Even if my people tried to visit me, they were not allowed in, except that once.

These people cause pain. In principle I believe that one should forgive, but it is difficult. I am not a racist; it is not a question of racial hatred. But the situation we live in is just so painful. We cannot forget it.

When I finished those 30 days, at the beginning of December, it was quite nice. Knowing that at least the next day I was going to eat meat or fish. Although food at Pretoria Prison is not what I would normally call edible. They prepare stuff which I think would make even a pig say no. And they expect a human being to be satisfied.

So every day, when they came for complaints, I kept telling them: 'You know, your food is terrible.'

They would reply, 'You know, Caesarina, *jy is nog nooit tevrede nie* [You're never satisfied].'

And I asked them, 'What is there to be satisfied about? Look at everything! One, I have never before come across soup made of pumpkin mixed with *samp* and a bit of fat and put salt there – you don't care, you only give it to us to keep us quiet. I am not in prison just to get fat on whatever; I do not want to be treated like a pig. And, secondly, if you can give your white prisoners properly prepared food, for sure I am entitled to that too.'

The complaints went round and round like a broken record. It is difficult for the apartheid gods to accept that a black person has the right to say no. Just as it is difficult for these same apartheid gods to accept, even today, that black people are going to rule South Africa tomorrow.

I lived on the third floor, in cell number one. The prison walls were once again all white, the floors were cement. There were three cells in a row, and then a small area, three by six metres. There was a grille and a steel door to enter this small space, then another grille and steel door to enter my cell. I once counted something like nine locked doors between me and the world outside.

There was a basin with cold and hot water and a toilet next to the basin, there was a wooden cupboard about two metres tall, and there was a bed, a bed with sheets, blankets, pillow and pillow-case.

But the real advantage of Pretoria was the windows. I had a window right at the top of my cell. That window you could easily open. And there was another window looking out towards the back, an outside window. I could climb on top of the cupboard and look out of it. Of course this was illegal, punishable, but I had to do it; I think it kept me sane. Looking through that window, seeing other people. It looked directly into the white male prisoners' hospital. And standing on top of the cupboard I could see 'maximum', the maximum security cells of the condemned prisoners. Such a long period, from 1976 up to the end of 1979, with only those few comrades' and warders' faces to study. Suddenly here I was able to see so many other people. Some were not even prisoners, but visitors going to maximum. You know, even if I could not talk to them, it made so much difference. I spent hours and hours gazing out of that window.

I think the stay at Pretoria helped me a lot. I was able to shake off the insanity I was developing at Kroonstad. Of course, both are prisons. But at Kroonstad they systematically and comprehensively deprived me, at Kroonstad they even went to the extent of painting the window panes white; I could only look into the white.

Most of my time in Pretoria I spent standing on the cupboard; looking at people in maximum, looking at white prisoners, sometimes singing to myself.

And at Pretoria Prison they gave me a bible. You know, I had never read the bible like I did then. For the whole two years I stayed in that prison I read only the bible. I read it from Genesis up to Revelations several times; I know it from the first page to the last; I can quote. Reading it was another way of keeping my mind together. I realised that this book was really dynamic. Certain chapters are just very good – Jeremiah, the Lamentations: 'Remember Oh Lord what has befallen us. Behold and see our disgrace. Our inheritance has been taken over.' It spoke to me, it speaks to us all.

During those first months in Pretoria I had to be strong, because here I was alone – I had lost my comrades at Kroonstad. They wanted to destroy me still – it was up to me to keep on resisting. They had never dealt with the issues we had raised; our problems still loomed large.

I could look at the white prisoners through the window. Some of them would be carrying fruits. And you just feel frustrated; we still had no fruits. Every one of them has fruits because he or she is white.

Kruger had refused to talk to us; Le Grange never gave us a direct answer. Even though they had transferred me to Pretoria, I took it to be my business to keep on complaining about the issues of food, of clothes, of equal treatment. One day I asked for writing paper. I wrote to Le Grange:

'By the way, you saw us in October; now we want to see the effect of this [meeting], because we complained about the treatment, about being discriminated against. That still continues, there has been no change whatsoever. I am still waiting for those fruits which we were complaining about then.'

After I had addressed the letter, I gave it to the prison authorities. After some three weeks, I questioned them: what did he say? They said that he had never replied. Heh, I got angry. So I asked for another piece of paper and wrote another letter. I wrote it to P. W. Botha himself. But I think the authorities only reacted by labelling this person a problem; it exposed me, alone, but still raising difficulties.

None the less, a person has to continue to resist to the very last, irrespective of the pressure that person is under. I felt it wise, necessary even, for me that the fight should not stop there. The issues are burning, a human being cannot just relax about them. They must know that even one woman alone will not simply submit to their so-called rules and regulations which they have devised only to oppress us.

And in time I found out I was not alone, that I was not the only one who was in isolation.

The section I was staying in had been designed for condemned prisoners. The cells below me, on the second floor, contained condemned women. One was Sheila from Rustenburg; the other was Caroline from Cape Town. Both of them were awaiting their appeals. One evening I heard a person singing in a very soft voice, singing a hymn. I started backgrounding that person, not knowing that this person was a condemned prisoner. We would sing hymns. She would wake up and sing in the middle of the night and I would hum with her.

After some time I asked one of the wardresses, 'By the way, who is singing every day, so sadly?'

I was told, 'She is one of the condemned prisoners. She is still waiting for her appeal.' They never liked her, you know; they were quite happy that if her appeal were to fail she would hang for what she did.

I felt that sentence, the death sentence. You are there, you get touched, listening to the condemned prisoners singing, seeing them through the windows, going through their exercises. You look at this person, knowing that she is supposed to die; that the apartheid regime has decided that on such and such a day they will take her soul from her body. My spirits soared when I heard that Sheila and Caroline had won their appeals. That at least these people had passed through this horror, of what must be the most testing experience in their lives. That now they would not be hanged.

One day, before they had won their appeals, I heard a lot of noise. Someone was protesting in Afrikaans: '*Ek wil dit nie doen ne. Niemand gaan my laat die kos eet* [I won't do it. No one is going to make me eat this].'

I knew the voice of the doctor and those of the medical people. They were trying to force her to eat her food. It was Caroline who was refusing to eat, yelling that she did not see the reason why she had to eat, since the apartheid regime had already decided to take her soul away. I think it was a week before the outcome of her appeal. From the wardresses I heard she was seriously losing weight; she had been on hunger strike for quite a long time. She was refusing to take a bath, refusing to talk to anyone. She just sat there, staring up. At one point the prison staff took the blankets from the cell; they would only give her the blankets in the evening because they feared she might commit suicide. But she won her appeal.

Caroline got 15 years on appeal and Sheila 27. Sheila's boyfriend was hanged. Both had been convicted for murdering 'madams' (their white employers).

Caroline had stolen money from the woman she was working for. This woman realised it, after some time, and threatened to call the police. But Caroline killed her instead. Sheila and her boyfriend had killed quite a number of people. They would rob and kill – they lived that way.

The two of them were taken away from that section after their appeals.

I saw Sheila only once, after she won her appeal. She was taken to isolation – she was on the one-day punishment they called 'three meal', meaning you got no food at all for three meals, one full day. I made it a strategy that I would sing, loudly, as I went down the passage and up the stairs for my exercise, so that other prisoners would know this Kona was coming. They would look out of their windows to see me. And that day Sheila looked out. I greeted her, this woman I had sung with so often but never met.

Another condemned prisoner came, a woman called Beatrice, originally from Soweto. Beatrice was a most stubborn prisoner. She had decided she was not going to speak to anyone. She did not talk, she did nothing. Beatrice did not act like Sheila and the others. The wardresses complained she beat them up.

Beatrice had been a domestic worker in Johannesburg. She told her boyfriend that this old woman, her employer, had a lot of money. So she and her boyfriend and her boyfriend's friend went for this woman, murdered her, put her in the bath and turned on the hot water. They boiled her, took the money and left. But Beatrice had forgotten that her reference book was there; they could trace her. She was pregnant when she was arrested and gave birth in prison. The boyfriend and the friend were hanged. After she was sentenced she was taken to Pretoria to hang; she lived directly beneath my cell. Beatrice won her appeal but she had gone totally mad by then, insane. Poor Beatrice, she was raving, uttering incomprehensible words, and the wardresses were scared to come near her. The only thing she could be heard crying for which made sense was her child, who had been taken away from her by a relative. None of her people came to visit her in death row. And this, I think, contributed to her insanity. She was later taken to a sanatorium.

On 9 November I heard someone calling me. I was singing, and somebody called my name. I answered, only to find that it was Tshidi. Tshidi and her aunt, Mrs Gumede, and Tshidi's mum all appeared on the same case, arrested for harbouring MK guerrillas. Tshidi's mother got a discharge, but Tshidi and her aunt were each sentenced to five years.

Tshidi's father was also a policeman and had worked together with my father. I had known her slightly, an acquaintance. She lived about five minutes' walk from my place in Mamelodi. We had lost touch with each other when I went to prison. But I had heard that Tshidi and her family were on trial. I was eager to hear the outcome.

So Tshidi called me. And I mean 'called', because we were far from each other, you know. There was a door in my cell with a grille. I would climb the grille up to the last bar, try to hold on to the window sills, open the glass panes of the top windows facing inside the prison. And scream to her. It was how we used to communicate, by shouting; we had no option.

I asked her, as I was in a single cell, whether she also stayed in a single cell. She said no, she was staying in a big cell. I asked her who she was with. She told me she was with her aunt, Mrs Gumede. I yelled: 'Hau, that's great. Pass my regards to her, just say hi!'

Her aunt tried to talk, but being an old lady in her sixties she could not shriek loudly enough.

We just had to talk to each other, whether or not they were listening. Asking questions – 'How are you? This one thing happened . . .' – that sort of thing. I was very happy. Here was a person, it's nice, man, a person I could speak sense to. Even if it was through bars, across the whole of Pretoria Prison.

In November, towards the end of the month, I was trying to call Tshidi and hai! somebody else answered. I shouted, 'Who are you?'

She answered 'I am Thandi.'

'Thandi who?'

And she said, 'Thandi Modise.' She said, 'How is it, Kona?'

I was puzzled. Here was a person who knew my name, my birthname Kona, not Caesarina, and I asked myself, 'But do I want to talk to this Thandi, man?' You know, you automatically get suspicious and think that maybe they are bringing in *agents provocateurs* to be with the common-law prisoners. So I asked her, 'Could you do me a favour? I want to talk to Tshidi.'

'Okay,' she replied, 'I'll do that.' And she called to Tshidi.

Tshidi responded. Tshidi said to me: 'You know what? She's Thandi, man!' and she tells me where Thandi comes from.

Aaiiee, it was nice. We were now increasing in number. We started talking. I was on the third floor right at the corner. Thandi was on the fourth floor, I think about thirty metres from my cell above me and 30 metres to the left. Also in solitary.

We were eager to communicate; we could shout. They would come and say, 'But you are making a noise, you know. The whole prison is listening to you.'

We argued, 'Whose fault is that?' I just said, 'Listen, it is not our fault. These are my friends and I must talk to them. There is only one solution, and the solution is an easy one. You unlock all these cells and we stay together. And we won't make a noise. But as you are locking me away like this, I am going to continue talking. And no one is going to stop me doing that, for sure.'

For quite a long time after Thandi arrived at Pretoria we did not see each other. But we made sure that every morning and every afternoon we would say hi to each other and do some talking.

87

About things in general. Sometimes you would discover a privilege had been taken away, the staff had done this or that. Being in the isolation section together lifted our morale.

When I asked Thandi why she was segregated, she said they had just told her to go to the isolation section when she arrived at the prison. And she stayed there for a considerable period of time. You know, I got to know Thandi then. Telling her about the comrades at Kroonstad when I left, some months back, now. She was eager to meet some of these people, too. At that time she was a newly convicted prisoner.

After some days, maybe in December, we were talking: 'What were you arrested for?' I asked her – I had not heard. She replied that she had been a student leader at Barolong, at Mafikeng, and she had skipped the country to go to Botswana. She turned down a scholarship and decided instead to go for MK. She had trained in Angola.

I was excited – a trained MK cadre, and a woman! She tried to describe the MK camps, but I could not build a picture of them. She recalled the comrade spirit of those camps, though. I promised her – shouting across the whole prison – that if I ever got out I intended to go for MK, too. The whole prison heard it.

When an aeroplane passed overhead, we would shout, 'SWAPO hit them hard – teach them a lesson they will never forget! Bloody bastards!'

We were still wearing the vests. And we had these red and white bedspreads. Thandi pulled the red cotton from the bedspread, smuggled in a needle – don't ask me how she managed to do that – and embroidered on her vest 'FREE ME' in red.

Some days after we had established contact, I decided to visit her cell. The wardresses came to let me out for exercise. I knew Thandi was on the fourth floor. They were expecting me to go straight to the exercise yard, but I zipped up the stairs, down the passage, and stood directly outside Thandi's cell. The wardresses were trailing after me – 'Caesarina, what are you doing?'

'Hey man, I want to see my sister. Understand me?' By then I was determined to do what I intended to do and to hell with the consequences. They had no more horrors to practise on me; they had tried everything they could, already.

I greeted her. It was good seeing this beautiful comrade, one of our heroines. We the generation of 1976, we admire the heroes and heroines of *Umkhonto We Sizwe*, the MK. I admired what Thandi had done; breaking away from the traditional role of the female in our society of supporting the male. Thandi Modise – a fully fledged soldier of the people.

For Christmas 1979 we stayed in segregation, isolation cells, in Pretoria Prison. At some stage in prison you get used to this Christmas thing; it is just one more Christmas, all you do is count the number of Christmases you have gone through.

At the beginning of 1980 Bongi, Fezi and Mancane were transferred to Pretoria Central Prison from Potchefstroom Prison. Bongi and Fezi were taken to the isolation section on arrival. Mancane joined Tshidi and Mama Gumede.

Sibongile Bongi Mthembu was a quiet, soft-spoken person in her twenties. She was arrested in 1977 and imprisoned for two years for sedition in May 1979. She was the only woman; seven out of the 11 accused were discharged and four were sentenced to either two or four years. During 1976 she was an activist in Soweto and was one of the executive members of the Soweto Student Representative Council. Her home was in Dlamini One, a district of Soweto.

Feziwe Fesi Bokolani was a nursing sister in Port Elizabeth before she was arrested in August 1978, convicted in May 1979 and sentenced to eight years. She won an appeal and her sentence was reduced to five years. She was married with one child. Her husband looked after their child while she was in prison. She completed her sentence in 1984. When I met her she was in her late thirties, a very nice person. She was arrested for recruiting people for military training.

Elizabeth Mancane Nhlapo was in her forties when I met her. She was arrested in November 1978 and was sentenced in March 1979 for recruiting people for military training. She was the mother of three school-age children. Her paternal aunt looked after her children during her absence. She was released in 1984. She is from Dlamini Three in Soweto.

Bongi wanted to know the procedure for washing our clothes. I told her that mine were washed twice a week. Apparently they were refused permission to get their clothes washed twice. They challenged this – and the prison staff decided to reverse everything in connection with my washing.

One day Erasmus came to me saying they were no longer going to wash my clothes twice a week because they had a lot of laundry to do. I wanted my clothes to be washed and ironed twice a week. I used to do that for myself in Kroonstad. Even when I was only wearing the pyjamas, petticoat and vest, I would change them every day and wash regularly. I like to be clean. In Pretoria, though, they take the clothes away to wash them. When I arrived they informed me that they were only going to wash my clothes once a week.

I replied, 'Okay, this is no problem for me. I mean, I can wash, I am not a cripple. What you can do is get me a laundry room, give me an ironing board, and I will do my own washing. No problem.'

They refused to do that. But I argued, and they compromised. Twice a week they took my clothing and my bedding, sheets, pillow-cases, to be washed and ironed and brought back to me. I did not know what the other comrades had arranged to be done, as I had gone straight to isolation.

There is one particularly stupid belief of many South African whites: that all blacks smell. It sits within the minds of these wardresses, that we are smelly. Fine: if we smell, whose fault is it? They use perfumes, they have all the showers and the baths, they can wash as many times as they want. But you take a common-law prisoner who is denied the opportunity of showering after working for them in prison. A prisoner must shower before six o'clock and be ready for parade; and he or she can wash again after close up. Don't forget that the majority of prisoners do not have the money to buy toiletries, that they do not have perfumes, roll-ons and all that. Here these common-law prisoners work in a laundry at Pretoria, this steaming place, doing washing for the very same people who tell them they are smelly.

If the common-law prisoners wanted their own clothes washed, they had to wash them in the cells. Then they would put their dresses on the floor and stamp and slide their feet across them, ironing the dresses with their feet. Every evening you would hear that, stamp and slide, stamp and slide; we called it '*uku gida*' (to dance). They would do this, and then these very same apartheid gods, who can't even wash their own panties, they take their panties to a laundry – they have the audacity to say we are smelly. It is one of those small things that make you sick of these people.

So I demanded that my clothes be washed twice a week, that whether I was in prison or what, I just had to be clean. And I was not going to *uku gida*. I told them, 'No, *ba hlanya* [they are mad]. I won't.'

So when Thandi arrived she asked me what the arrangement was about washing clothes. I told her that my clothes were taken twice a week and returned properly washed and ironed. Thandi then had some problems with these characters – they tried to insist upon washing her clothes once a week – but eventually they conceded for her, too.

Serious problems started when Feziwe, Bongi and Elizabeth Nhlapo arrived. At this point the warders said that they had a lot of work and would only wash their clothes once a week; that that was final. The other comrades challenged them, saying that it was funny Caesarina was getting clean clothes twice a week, why not them?

All of a sudden they declared that I also was not going to get clean clothes twice a week. I agreed, saying: 'That is best; then I will go back to my old self. If you are stubborn, I can be stubborn. Fine, so I won't put the clothes on. Until you have the common sense to realise that I wish to be treated like a human being. I know how to wash and how to iron, I can do that for myself. But you think that by giving me time to wash and iron my clothes I won't feel the isolation. So I'll do this until you find some common sense.'

And I kept to my policy. I did not put the clothes on. It was another clothing strike. I wore only my nightdress. After a couple of days they realised this was another case.

I told the head of the prison, 'You know, you people, it is difficult for you to see that we mean business here. Don't think that we are clowning. Either you have common sense or we will have to put common sense into your minds.'

The other comrades had problems; their clothes were dirty and they did not know what to do. I showed them, 'Hey you guys, look here! Me, I am on strike.'

After a few days Bongi joined the strike and we proceeded. And the others joined too.

The apartheid rulers leave you with no alternative but action, direct action. They do not understand anything verbal. If you know why you are there, why you are in prison, you will know that you cannot just lie down for them to sit on top of you. That strike turned into another victory; the comrades won. We all got the same treatment, even those who did not participate in the strike; our clothes were cleaned.

I had yet more problems with the prison staff people. Because of the complaints I lodged they increased the time of exercise to an hour. So they used to give me exercise from 10 to 11. I walked out to the fourth floor, where there was a little courtyard where we took exercise. At 11 I returned to my cell for the meal; they were supposed to give me the food right at the door of the cell. Unlock the door, hand the food over to you.

One Saturday I went out for exercise. But instead of taking the food to my room and handing it to me, they left the plate on the passage floor. When I walked in from the exercise yard, into the passage leading to my room, the wardress commented, 'Ah, Caesarina. There is your food.'

'No, I don't take my food here. I expect my food to be given to me in my room.'

She started with 'We must ask you to speak to . . .' but I interrupted. 'Oh, stop clowning. I expect my food to be right in my cell, not here.' I walked down the passage, past the food and into the cell.

The following day I launched a complaint that I did not get my food, that I was still waiting for yesterday's lunch. That happened five times; some days they put my food on the floor and I ignored it.

I asked the comrades how was lunch; they told me they had eaten meat. I shouted to Thandi, *'Thandi, mchana, ho jeloe eng kajeno? We tseba batho ba haba moneya dijo?* [Thandi, comrade, what did you eat today? You know, these people never gave me food today?]'

She came back with, 'We ate delicious meat. What happened?' I explained that the lunch had been left in the passage and that they wanted me to pick it up off the floor. My comrades were adamant: 'No, *mchana*, you must never do that.'

The person behind the whole thing was that Sergeant Kekana; it seemed that one day I was going to lose my temper with her, yerrah. The fifth time this occurred was on a Good Friday. I had come back from exercise, and there was this wardress who was working under Kekana, putting my food in the passage yet again. 'Caesarina, here is your food.'

I replied as usual, 'Aaiiee, you expect me to eat my food here? I expect it to be in the room.' This time I wanted to beat her up.

She walked away. 'Let me go and call Kekana.' And when Kekana came, even she could tell I was really angry and intended to fight. So Kekana backed off: 'Okay, I'll bring your food to you.' Then she went and did not come back with the food.

I began to rage. Bongi, Feziwe and Thandi called out, 'What's happening?'

'These people, it seems they are getting too funny. Because they have not brought me my lunch.'

Thandi asked, 'Ah, *le kajeno ha wa ja?* [Today you do not eat, too?]'

'No, it's okay, *ketlaba bona* [I'll see to them].'

At supper time Kekana came to me again in the company of another sergeant. She brought me my supper. I took the plate and put it on top of the cupboard. She was supposed to give me medicine first, né? But instead of taking the medicine from her I went for her. 'I want my lunch. I want my lunch. I am sick and tired of this nonsense. Every time. This is the fifth time I have not got my food. I mean, I must just show you what I mean physically because when I talk to you politely you think that I am a fool; you think that oh well, I won't do anything. So I will have to show you that I can do something.'

We began to hit each other. The other sergeant tried to assist Kekana, of course, but I gave her a clap and she ran away up the stairs, like she was going for ever. Kekana and I were fighting, hey! Smashing each other. Eventually she broke out of my hands and ran up the stairs after her sergeant, and I returned to my cell.

After some time a certain wardress showed up with my medicine. Now that one was a real hypocrite. She pretended all was fine. I just looked and ignored her. After some ten minutes the head of the prison, whom we called Mokoko, came – in the company of three men. They locked the grille, and they locked the door, and they left.

The following morning, they were supposed to bring my breakfast. They unlocked the door, and they unlocked the grille, and there was the plate sitting on the passage floor. They said 'Okay, here is your food.' And they left the grille and the door open for me to take my bath.

I walked out to the bathroom, took my bath, then headed straight back into my cell. The food stayed there on the floor. It was another action, another hunger strike. If there was one thing they ought to have known by then, it was that I was good at hunger strikes. But some people have to learn the hard way.

For four days I did not eat. They would unlock the cell and then, breakfast, lunch and supper, leave the food on the cell floor. And I would leave it there, too. They would come back and take it away, untouched.

On the fourth day I took my medicine from the man who brought it, looking him in the eye. And he asked, 'Why are you looking at me like this?' I just looked at him, shook my head and went back inside my cell. They tried to provoke me and failed; they felt small. I decided this time I would discipline them by keeping quiet. It frustrates them: when they expect you to talk, you say nothing, silence, just look at them; and when they expect you to

93

keep quiet, then you go for them.

The doctor came. He also wanted to know why I would not eat. So I told him: 'Your people are treating me like a dog. I am not a dog, you cannot put my food on the floor. And if you are not willing to treat me like a human being, fine, I won't take your stuff. And that is that.'

The doctor could not understand that refusal to take my food off the floor. I set him a simple question: 'Would you like to be treated like that?'

He replied, 'I would not, but this is prison.'

'There is nothing like "but this is prison!" I would rather be treated like a human being, not just like a dog.'

I suspect he was the person who brought it up with the authorities: 'This person is serious about going on hunger strikes, until we decide to behave like normal people.' For on the fifth day my food was properly handed to me by the wardress. Fine. It was grand. I resumed eating.

That same Kekana later fought with MaTau, who was serving some years for theft. MaTau was in isolation; she stormed at Kekana, fought them, fought their men as they put her into a straitjacket. And MaTau's hatred for Kekana remained; that Kekana had to be solved. You know, we often learn that these very same characters who are collaborating, informing on our comrades, are ill-treating the whole of our people. You ask yourself the question, does this person know that one day we are going to take over? Where will he or she be? Because we are not fighting a struggle without ending. Every one of us knows that takeover is inevitable. So where is Kekana going to be then? And the many other Kekanas?

Because they had taken away all my so-called privileges, there was nothing I could use for my body, like a lotion or anything for the skin. My face got really bad; I looked terrible. I was using margarine. Margarine is not good for a person's face, of course, but I used it because for two years and six months there was nothing I could put on to moisturise my skin. Just to keep a bit of oil on it, just to keep it from cracking. And it looked terrible, with a lot of pimples. So one day when I was having a bath, I wailed, 'Hey hey he, *unzima lomthwalo*! [The load is heavy!]' I couldn't believe what I saw in the mirror.

Feziwe's cell was right on top of mine. She laughed, you know. And I could not work out what she was laughing at. After they had locked us up for lunch, she called me.

'Kona!'

'How's it?'

'Ah, grand.'

She said, 'Hey hey hey, *unzima lomthwalo!*'

And I echoed '*Unzima, m'chana, unzima unzima blind* [It's difficult comrade, it's extremely difficult].'

She asked curiously, 'Why did you say so?'

'I was looking at my face, man. And then I realised that aaiiee, *unzima*, aaiiee, *ufuna madoda*, straight.'

I am not trying to be a materialist, but you just have to be strong to survive under the conditions we were in. We were suffering there, without all those things a person in this world likes to have and takes for granted. And if you are not strong – ah, forget it. Sometimes we have only ourselves, our own words and songs, our own beliefs, to help us survive.

In Pretoria Prison I used to sing a lot. When I went our for exercise I would go up the stairs to the fourth floor and I would sing. That annoyed them. After I had been singing like that for some weeks they announced it was against the law. 'Caesarina, you are not supposed to sing. It is against the rules and regulations for a prisoner to sing, even to whistle. It is punishable. From such a period to such a period, you are not supposed to sing aloud.'

I got very angry; I think it was the only freedom I was left with. I replied, 'You know, I am not surprised, because everything a person does in this country is against the law. Even our existence is against the law, black people's existence is against the law. All these stupid rules and regulations, everything you are trying to do, no matter how innocent a thing it might be, it is against the law. What is not against the law? If you know anything, just anything which is not against the law, please let me know.'

So that day during exercise time I sang, very loud. This just made them mad. But perhaps they had finally learned one lesson: punishing me would not solve the actual problem. They learned they had to give in on some of these rules and regulations. They could only repeat: 'Caesarina, you are not supposed to sing; you are supposed to exercise.'

'Okay, what is the meaning of exercise? Am I not supposed to exercise my lungs?' And I sang even more loudly than before. The wardress looked at me in silence. One needs strong lungs for the struggle ahead, after all – 'VICTORY IS CERTAIN!'

Twelve

On my arrival at Pretoria, I met quite a number of prisoners, common law as well as political. Communication was by calling each other, shouting loud. Most of them lived on the first floor, the isolation section. There was one comrade called Bongani from East London. She was a very miltant comrade and I liked her very much. Immediately after my arrival at Pretoria, as I've said, I began singing, and she was the unknown voice who seconded my singing. She had been convicted for sabotage, doing two years in, with four years suspended. She was a tough lady, a tough comrade.

There was this tendency during the 1976,1977,1979 period for many comrades to be treated like common-law prisoners, rather than be placed with the political prisoners. Lunka Nyamza was one of them. She was a student activist from Mdansane, a township outside King William's Town, and was sentenced to two years for participating in public disturbances.

One Sunday, during church services, they sang this hymn: '*Jerusalem, ikhaya lam*' . . . ', but the lyrics were changed and were sung in the revolutionary manner:

> *South Africa ikhaya lam'*
> *endili thandayo* (twice)
> *Sizo wulwel' 'mhlaba wethu*
> *kuze sikhululeke* (twice)

> [South Africa the home
> that I love (twice)
> We shall fight for our land
> until freedom comes (twice)]

The wardresses in the church service spied on her, reported her, and she was taken to isolation; thus I met her. During the day they would take her to work, and at night take her back to isolation, because they did not want her to stay with other common-law

96

prisoners. They said she had some influence over them. They gave her a very rough time.

We had another comrade from Port Elizabeth, named Ntombisa. She was also arrested for participating in student protests and she was serving two years. During that period when Lunka was kept in isolation, at least Ntombisa managed to stay in the big cell with the other common-law prisoners. Some time after Lunka left, she was also taken to isolation. Her case was treated as though it were a common crime, like a criminal case. When we met she had seven months of her sentence still to go.

Ntombisa went to isolation because she was always stopping to talk with me whenever we had a chance to talk. They said she was getting tainted. She had once asked me, shouting, whether I was working, and I had explained to her: 'No, I'm not working. I find no reason why I should work. I do not know why I was arrested. I'm not a criminal.'

The following day she refused to work. She got 20 days in isolation because of that.

Shouting at each other across the isolation block, we got to know each other well. We taught each other political songs. Some days the prison walls just echoed defiance, back and forth: oppression or no oppression, exploitation or no exploitation, imprisonment or no imprisonment, *a luta continua*, until final victory.

Singing happened with common-law prisoners as well. Singing helps keep people sane. And they used to sing well. They would start immediately after lock-up. A person like me, liking music, I appreciated that. At least you could hear sounds from various sections, unlike Kroonstad where there was nothing, totally nothing; there we were really isolated.

Most of the condemned prisoners would sleep during the day and during the night they would sing. Very late in the night, maybe one or two in the morning, you would hear them singing. And you would know that these people were going to hang.

When you look in South Africa's prisons, you find the majority, 90 or 95 per cent, of the condemned prisoners are black. If a black man rapes a white woman, he is going to hang. But if a white man rapes a black woman, he may get a very light sentence – even as little as a 30 rands' fine. You know, they treat us as though we are not human, as if our mothers just picked us up off the trees, like picking a fruit. The way they treat us, you would think our mothers never felt the pain, that they did not suffer at all bringing us up. For them, it is only whites in South Africa whose parents cared when they brought them into the world.

We heard condemned prisoners from the male section singing revolutionary songs. Their favourite was *Unzima lomthwalo*. I did not know at that time who they were. Later I found out that they were Motaung, Mogoerane, Mosolodi and Shabangu.

Motaung had been a student at Diepkloof Secondary before leaving the country to join the people's army. He was arrested for ANC activities and sentenced to death. One of 11 children, he was 28 years old when executed on 9 June 1983.

Mosolodi was a student in form 3 at Orlando North High before he left the country to join *Umkhonto We Sizwe*. He was arrested for ANC activities and sentenced to death. He, too, was executed on 9 June 1983 by the racist regime.

Mogoerane was from Boksburg and was 23 when he was sentenced to death for ANC activities. The apartheid gods hanged him also on 9 June 1983.

Shabangu was aged 23 and came from Middleburg in the Transvaal. He was sentenced to death but this was later commuted to a life sentence. He was involved in the Silverton Siege.

To be honest, looking at the situation, I personally think blacks in South Africa have all the right to hate; but because we are human we have to live together in peace – we must work together. We can only do that when we get rid of the evil system of apartheid, totally and forever.

The apartheid regime makes a lot of money out of prisoners. They use the prisoners as free labour. Pretoria Prison runs a commercial laundry using black prisoners' labour. On the ground floor there is a large laundry, with big machines and all that, where thousands of articles are washed and ironed daily. You find that these bastards are making thousands of rands a month out of our sisters here. Eighty or 85 per cent of the common-law prisoners in Pretoria work in that laundry. You find that police stations, the entire prison staff, the army, and even private people all send their laundry there to be washed. And they pay very little to have it done. These apartheid gods enjoy their cheap labour. They just take a lot of prisoners, lock them up, the prisoners do their washing, and they pay far less than they would normally.

Some short-term prisoners are 'sold' to work as labourers for the Boers. I have never heard of a case of a black man going to the prison authorities to buy a prisoner this way; it is always whites who do this, and mostly farmers. They take these poor prisoners, often people who have broken some pass law, and make them work for 50 cents a day.

So often, really cruel whites abuse this prison labour terribly. There was one incident while I was at Pretoria Prison where one woman prisoner ran away from the place where she was working, sewing for some white woman. She had been serving six months, and they had threatened to double her sentence if she ran away and was caught. But this woman who hired her from the prison was so cruel. So the woman decided to run away and come back to this prison. Working for this woman must have been miserable if she thought Pretoria Prison was an improvement. And that particular day it was raining heavily, too; she stood outside the prison gates, on the street, soaking, until the rain had stopped. Some of the prison staff members found her there outside the walls and took her in. She fell seriously ill as a result of this.

I also managed to communicate with a number of the ordinary common-law prisoners, usually those on the isolation block. Most of them had already heard of me, this Caesarina. They wanted to get to know me. As for me, these were my sisters; I just had to talk to them.

I came to know some of them fairly well, and I liked them. I felt that most just needed direction – if they managed to get sufficient direction, a clear political line, they would be dynamite. People have respect for those who resist; prisoners in Pretoria respected our cause, our struggle. Our resistance was so high; they would tell us, 'You are taking the frustration away from us, you are getting it tough there, at the top.'

I made it a point to follow up some of these women after our release, not just to leave them in limbo. What we have to ask is: why are these people in prison? Why are these mothers spending so many years locked up? Every South African has a role to play in our liberation struggle. It is for us to educate these people.

Of the women I came across in prison, some are today in our women's group in Mamelodi. Some of them are on the executive. They are just dynamite, as I had thought.

For instance, take a person like Mama Joanna, together with her two daughters, two sons and her husband. She was serving 15 years, and her two daughters were each serving seven years. Or a person such as Aus Sheila, serving three years. Or Photu, serving four years, or Lavi, serving three years. Leaving their kids at home, with no one to support them, to look after them. And you look at the cause, at why these people have to serve these sentences. The fact that they commit a crime and land in prison is only incidental. Look at the real causes. Some of our people cannot get work, because of the pass laws. Some of our people cannot get work because they are illiterate. Some cannot get employment because they are not supposed to be in the particular area they live in. Or people can only find jobs that leave them broken; farm jobs, mining jobs, domestic worker jobs. We cannot punish crimes committed in order to survive, crimes committed in order to live a little better in this painful life we are forced into. South African prisons are so full because of the injustices against our people.

We cannot attend to the effect only. Definitely not. It is for us, for every single person in South Africa, irrespective of colour, creed or class, to fight against this evil system. To fight for a non-racial, united South Africa. To fight for a South Africa owned by the people. This is the policy of my organisation, the African National Congress, and I respect it. The people must govern; not a handful of apartheid gods. It is then that we can solve some of these problems.

Our most basic document is the Freedom Charter, printed at the beginning of this book. Look at one of the simple statements. 'There shall be houses, security and comfort.' You find that thousands of people, millions even, in South Africa do not have houses today. That millions of people in South Africa live in shacks, under plastic material stretched as roofs, or tin-tacked together; while the white minority live in beautiful houses. Until we answer such a simple demand we will never find peace in my war-torn country.

Look at the students fighting today for equal education. The apartheid regime claims they have 'reformed' education, but we still find a coloured education, an Indian education, a black education, a white education. We do not want this; we want to see one education for all, where every student is catered for, where every student knows that this is our education, not their education. The Freedom Charter demands: 'The doors of learning and culture shall be opened.' To everyone.

I had not been born when the regime introduced Bantu education. Our fathers, our mothers, our heroes fought and died, to stop this evil system. I was only a student in 1976. We found ourselves in the streets again, fighting this same Bantu education. We found ourselves serving sentences because of this.

This apartheid has brought misery to the people of South Africa. It is for us to stop that.

Most of the common-law prisoners in Pretoria Prison were arrested for theft. I spoke to them, passing time, and this was done mostly during the night. Immediately after lock-up (our night starts at four in the afternoon), we were communicating with each other, asking why was the other in prison, and all that. Almost all that I spoke to were arrested for stealing something from shops or for pickpocketing; only a few had been engaged in major robbery. You try to gauge their feelings about it – 'Can you tell me why? Couldn't you find work?' A person would tell you, 'Even if I find work, how much do they pay me?'

You find that a lot of them are illiterate. And they tell you: '*MaBoru ba re ja matsogo* [We are exploited],' that they would prefer to go and steal because they think that way they can make ready cash, and fast.

Today, that system is trying to teach white youths that they should be ready to die on the borders or in our townships, that they should get shot in order to preserve whites' swimming pools. The system tries to teach them to be prepared to die for that luxury life. All we are asking is to live like human beings, to determine our own lives, to have a chance to live. And these same people call themselves Christians. It is a heartbreaking situation, a frustrating situation. It needs all of us to attend to the problem. To uproot this miserable system, to put the people in power. The people must have a say.

On one occasion in Pretoria Prison everyone received porridge that had clearly gone completely off. I complained about it, but nothing was done. The situation reached the point where I said I would not taste this porridge. I gave it back to them, only to find that all the prisoners throughout the prison were complaining. We asked if this was the last mealie meal left in the country, intended for feeding the pigs, that they had decided to cook to feed to us. And this was not said by political prisoners; it was said by common-law prisoners.

I refused to take the porridge. And taking note of my past record they agreed to give me oats. But the rest of the prison continued to receive that porridge which was off.

Two days later, after complaining and complaining without result, the common-law prisoners decided they had to boycott this food. The porridge was dished up, and no one touched it. The head of the prison called in the lieutenant in charge of the kitchen. They could not believe common-law prisoners would revolt like this. But here they were faced with a hunger strike of more than 200 prisoners. This lieutenant stormed in shouting: '*Die een wat brom sluit hom toe. Die een wat kaak praat sluit hom toe. Ek kook die pap van half drie tot half ses, hulle sê die pap is nie gaar nie? Sluit hom toe!* [The one who complains, lock him up. The one who talks shit, lock him up. I cook this porridge from from half past three to half past six, and they say this porridge is not well cooked. Lock him up!]' He was vicious, acting as though he would beat up every single prisoner, personally.

With the common-law prisoners, however, there is a serious lack of purpose. Also, they, at least, have the possibility of parole; and if you misbehave you most definitely do not get that parole. So some try to be nice and turn into informers, getting other people into trouble, hoping to build a very clean record.

The ringleaders were singled out and bundled off to isolation. These people went on spare diet for leading that hunger strike.

Once again, as so often happened, the apartheid gods were not in the least bit willing to listen to genuine grievances of the people. That is precisely why we see South Africa burning today. Millions of people have grievances which need attention, which have to be dealt with. But ask yourself the question: who is willing to listen to them, to resolve these grievances? Not the system, not the government. In fact they take those people who are protesting to be trouble-makers. People who say no to apartheid, people who say no to oppression and exploitation, these people are regarded as communists. And they argue that South Africa is burning today only because of these agitators, these people whom they call communists. They treat us like this, with all our misery in this country, and then they tell the world that it is only some agitators who have made the place burn. I am telling you that with that kind of stupid approach they are going to have ashes.

When I went out for exercise they made all the other prisoners, the common-law prisoners, go away and hide themselves somewhere. I do not know whether the authorities thought that a person with an infectious disease was coming out for exercise or what, but that was the way they normally dealt with political prisoners. They failed to realise that treating them like this would in fact make the poor common-law prisoners more inquisitive. Some of them who had recently been convicted would wonder 'But why are we hiding when this person is supposed to go out?'

And I used to make it deliberate policy that when I saw a prisoner, any prisoner, I would walk straight up to her and greet her: 'How's it?'

'Fine thanks, and you?'

'Ah, grand.'

This made the staff mad. And they could not stop it. The only thing they could think of doing was to hide the prisoners from me, when they could. So I would proceed like that, deliberately – not forgetting that some of these people were from around my home. Pretoria Prison contains mostly prisoners from around Pretoria, and some knew me. I could ask about people I knew, how this one or that one was.

I tried to break down these attempts to cut us off from the common-law prisoners, to divide us from the people. We were all prisoners together, irrespective of what we had been imprisoned for. How should we behave? Should we accept the walls they try to build up beween us? We could not allow this to happen. We had to show that we were resisting these divisons, that we were one.

Whether common-law prisoners or whatever, we are all trapped in a political dilemma. Therefore, I say, all prisoners, black and white, are political prisoners, irrespective of the crimes that land us in the prison. It is the system that makes people hungry and illiterate. It makes people desperate. Desperate people do desperate things and in this desperation we land up in places like this – in prison. It is our future, for all of us.

They may try to prove that they have all the power; but we know that our unity is strength. In the end, the survival of the South African people lies with all of us in this country – it is for us, all of us, to get rid of this regime. We must uproot this apartheid, this divide and rule, this separate development.

So in prison we tried our level best to bring common-law prisoners closer to us. They came to feel that we were fighting for them, that they were part and parcel of the struggle. And that we were not angels, that we needed them to fight this enemy with us, we needed them to help to challenge, to resist, to protest against the apartheid regime.

When common-law prisoners were sentenced to 30 days' spare diet punishment they would come to our isolation block. We would smuggle sugar to them, so that they could at least have something to eat with their porridge. Eventually most of the prisoners knew that if they went for isolation, there were people at the top who were trying to do something for them – meaning other prisoners on the top floors of the prison in isolation, not the wardresses who thought they were sitting on top of our heads.

It was a nice thing. They would get the sugar, use it for porridge.

They did not feel they were alone; they knew that their sisters were there, who felt for them, who sacrificed for them. And also that we wanted their confidence, their support.

To be honest, I am sure that we succeeded in educating prisoners in Pretoria and later in Klerksdorp Prison. Such prisoners had been given a wrong picture about us. Fortunately we succeeded in proving to the common-law prisoners that we were there because we fought for everyone in the country, every single person. We were fighting for their future, too. Our future, all of us.

Thirteen

Finally, after a long struggle, the issue of our segregation was taken up outside the prison walls. I think the person who really assisted us here was Bongi. She was released from prison, directly from segregation into the outside world. She was able to bring the attention of the world outside to us, was able to reach the people who had been ignorant of what was happening to us, despite the publicity surrounding the Kroonstad case.

It seems people were under the impression that after the Kroonstad case the authorities had ended segregation, when in fact a person like me still remained in segregation. So Mrs Jana, the political lawyer, instructed lawyers to take up the case, to lay a charge against the Prisons Department for keeping us in segregation unlawfully. It became topical; it was a cause.

Mrs Suzman, the well-known liberal MP, came to visit us, too. She is the long-standing opposition member of the Progressive Federal Party. For years she was a lone voice in the South African Parliament. Her party is against racism. She saw us all together: Tshidi, Mama Gumede, Elizabeth Nhlapo, Thandi, Feziwe and me. We were taken to Lieutenant Bothma's office. We were sitting in that office, and they put these cakes on the table. Maybe they were trying to be nice to Helen Suzman. Or maybe they were trying to imply that we ate cakes all the time. All the time we were telling her about this terrible food we were expected to eat, this terrible treatment we received, we were watching these cakes in front of us, which we couldn't touch.

We told her everything, in detail. She was stunned. She could not believe it, that anyone could live in segregation for so long, without visits, without reading material, without anything except the bible. With only herself to talk to. When she came I had already been in segregation for more than two years.

Mrs Suzman even went to the extent of suggesting that a psychiatrist should come to see me. But the unfortunate part of this was that she did not tell me, she did not tell any of us, that she planned to do this. She proposed this when she got back outside.

So the following week I saw a psychiatrist. This was a woman, white of course, maybe in her late forties, an Afrikaner. I understand she lectured at Pretoria University. By that time I assumed anyone who came saying 'I am from one two three, I have been sent to do this this this' to be part and parcel of the apartheid regime. Eh, I was furious, burning mad. Did they now think that I was crazy?

This psychiatrist started by asking me questions such as who I was, where I was from, why I was in prison and what tribe I belonged to. Yerrah ma, I hit the roof! How could she come and ask me about what tribe I belonged to, what language I spoke at home? Did she think I didn't know why I was in prison? Besides, whoever told her that I wasn't normal? I was angry because first these people had put me into segregation for so long a period and then they brought this character here to ask me stupid questions, implying I must be insane.

I said to her, 'I am South African you know; I do not have a special tribe. I speak all the languages and belong to all the tribes.' Because they like to encourage tribalism. They like you to believe you come from this group or that group, and you are therefore not a South African but only a Sotho or a Swazi or a Xhosa. Which is something we must avoid at all costs.

And I asked her whether those who had sent her had told her that they did not give me certain foods. There were certain types of food they did not give me because I was black. Was she aware there was a lot of discrimination in prison?

And she told me that she was there to speak to me as a psychiatrist. I repeated, 'But what about the problems I am facing here? I am telling you there is a lot of apartheid. And if you see to that, there will not be any problems. As for me, I am very normal.'

I suggested that she attend to the apartheid gods, not to me.

105

Anyone can see that they are so insane, their insanity cannot be controlled. No normal person would promote racial discrimination; these mad men who rule our country have made racial discrimination the law of our land. A psychiatrist might be useful in treating those mad apartheid gods.

And I told her that I no longer wished to see her. That was on the first day.

The next day I saw our lawyer together with the other comrades. He had a newspaper cutting from the Sunday papers; on the second page there was this statement that Helen Suzman had visited us, and that it was she who had recommended that this woman come to see me, because she felt it was completely destructive of a person's mentality to remain in segregation for such a long period of time. After seeing him, after we had told him the story from A to Z, we were taken back to our various cells.

And when they locked me into my cell that day I announced: 'Hey you guys, look here, I want to see that psychiatrist character again.' The head of prisons said: 'But Caesarina, you just chased her away.'

I said: 'Listen, you have to understand that I have the right to change my mind at any time. As long as I think that this is right for me, I can do that. So you call her, I want to see her.'

The psychiatrist came again. 'But you said you did not want to see me again.'

I replied, 'No, that shows I am normal. I have the right to change my mind at any time.' And I asked her, 'Did you tell them that I want fruits, huh?'

We just sat there; we did not speak to each other for more than ten minutes. She was confused, because I only repeated what I had told her on the previous visit, about the discrimination and all that. I was sticking to these points. It was clearly difficult for her to say anything.

She tried to act like a psychiatrist, tried to get me into a corner. She asked me to tell her why I was convicted.

'That has nothing to do with you.'

She thought that she could prove to me that if you were doing one two three, and it was illegal, you would receive punishment, you had to take the consequences. She wanted to justify the segregation to me, to show that it was because I was so uncooperative that I was treated in this way. She put it: 'If you are uncooperative, then this this and this,'

I wish I knew who had taught them that word, 'uncooperative'.

106

Honestly, just why should I co-operate with them? They are doing such things to us that we have no choice as human beings but to oppose them, and then they complain that we are uncooperative.

While I was speaking to her they served lunch to the prisoners. White prisoners passed the office with their white lunch. That time it was peanut butter, bread, fruit. The door was open and we could both see it. I showed her: 'You see, that is what I have been telling you. When I return to my cell I won't see that food, I won't see that peanut butter, because I'm black. What do you say? Do you think I'm right? I tell you that you have to attend to those problems, because there is no sanity in this country. They cannot expect sanity in this prison while there is this discrimination against most of us here.'

She left. I never saw that woman again.

The publicity had its effect. Feziwe and Thandi were taken out of segregation. The very same day, before they told the two comrades that they were leaving the isolation section, Sergeant Erasmus picked a quarrel with me, a heated quarrel. I was having a shower, and while I was in the middle of it she came in: 'Exercise!' I was affronted. 'Hai, stop clowning. How can you expect me to get out of the bath and start doing exercise. I am not yet through with the bathing.'

'Anyway, you have forfeited your exercise, then.'

I warned her. 'You people do not want peace; you are inviting a fight. Recently I have realised that there is one thing you are inviting. You will really get it; I am going to *donner* [beat] you.'

This woman knew that they were about to inform my other two comrades, Feziwe and Thandi, that the following day they would be removed from isolation section, to stay with the other comrades. She knew that the segregation was due to end the next day.

But when these comrades called to me, 'Kona, do you know that today our segregation is terminated?' I could only reply, 'Hau!' They were both shocked to find I had not been told. They had been aware of the quarrel that morning – but there was nothing they could do.

The following morning they were taken to stay with the other comrades. I was left alone.

I told myself: 'I do not care what happens to me. They will not break me. I will keep on resisting. I mean I am not going to buy the termination of my segregation with my soul. So they can keep it.' That was that.

107

I stayed in segregation several more weeks. In the afternoon, after lock-up, my comrades could call to me across the sections.

'How's it?'

'I'm all right, and how are you there?'

During the day my comrades were working, which is something I would never agree to do. They were doing needlework. Since 1979 I had made it absolutely clear that as far as I was concerned, aaiiee, forget it. I wouldn't work until I was released; I wouldn't work for them. It was against my principles to work in prison. But I felt bad about my comrades.

Towards the end of September I heard a serious quarrel. I was in the dark, alone in my single cell, hearing doors slamming, screams, all that, and batons at work. I found that my comrades had complained about the food, that it was not properly prepared and that it was not sufficient.

Soon after, I think around 27 or 28 September, my comrades called me to tell me that Feziwe had been taken away. I asked where to? They did not know; they suspected it must be Klerksdorp or Pollsmoor. Eh, now what were they trying to do to us?

On 30 September, all my comrades – Thandi, Tshidi, Elizabeth Nhlapo, Elisabeth Gumede – were dragged into single cells, forcibly. They shouted this to me. 'Aaiiee, *mchana*, we are in segregation!'

'Hau, what is happening now?'

'Né, these people are trying to keep us one in each cell.'

'Why . . . ?'

'They say that when we are together we create more problems.'

The next day, on 1 October 1981, they took me from one single cell directly to another single cell.

Then I complained. 'Hey you characters, ah, you guys, what is this? Are you telling me you have taken me out of segregation? I want to stay with the other comrades.'

'Which comrades?'

'My other comrades – Feziwe, Thandi, Elisabeth Gumede, Elizabeth Nhlapo, Tshidi.'

They merely said: 'They are all in single cells. You can meet when you are doing exercise.' And they added, 'Okay, we don't mind taking you to a big cell – you can stay in there alone.'

So I remained in a single cell, this time on the fourth floor. There are certain issues in life which you eventually decide it is futile to argue about.

They were finally persuaded to take me out of segregation, but they only did this after they had removed all comrades from the big

108

room and had put them into single cells. These people appeared to be unwilling to see me staying in a big cell together with other comrades. From my first days in prison, for the whole six years I was inside, I remained in single cells. I never did stay in a cell with other comrades. Even before the segregation at Kroonstad, we would move together during the day, work together, and return each to her own cell at locking-up time. I had become used to it, it did not bother me so much. It was just this question: Why me?

At least during exercise time we could at least meet, face to face, and talk normally. After that, everyone to her cell. The end of segregation meant we could meet for exercise, we could get library books, we could buy toiletries.

We were staying on the same passage. Tshidi's cell was second from the corner, mine was the fifth, Mama Gumede's was the ninth – a long way down, and all still in the isolation section. Sometimes other common-law prisoners would be placed in the cells in between, for punishment. Thandi stayed on the same floor, but down a different passage.

The other comrades continued working during the day. I started reading library books. They were not great literature, but at least they were something different from the bible, which I had been through over and over, for two years, non-stop.

One day I asked for writing paper, to write to my cousin. I wrote her a nice letter. In that letter I referred to two verses in the bible. I quoted Jeremiah 50 and 51. I gave the staff the letter to post. The following day they told me I would not be allowed to send this type of letter; here was another piece of paper and I could write another letter.

'What is wrong with that letter?'

'You are not supposed to quote the bible.'

I wrote another letter. Supposedly that letter was directed to my cousin, but the content of the letter was aimed at the prison staff. I went home on that piece of paper, you know. I really get irritated with these characters, who call themselves Christians on days when it suits them. Here they are, stopping me from quoting that very same bible which they brought to the South African people, that very same bible which they were so happy for me to read, for years on end, and nothing else. So I made sure that letter was quite undesirable. They did not send it.

We got a visit from two judges. When they came, we were busy doing exercises. The judges asked for complaints. We had yet another complaint about the meat; they still tried to punish people with food, even when they knew comrades would revolt. Like I said before, they are not sane.

During that visit from the judges, one lawyer asked Mama Gumede why she was in prison – particularly at her age. She said, no, she did not know why she was arrested. He was incredulous. 'Are you telling me that you were picked up for no reason?'

She answered, 'No. These characters came to my place to arrest me because they said I did not come to report my son to them. He was back from exile. Me, I do not have any politics at all.'

Unfortunately, minutes after this sweeping pronouncement, Mama Gumede was complaining: 'And you know, these people are treating us badly, like people in Cambodia.'

'Oh, I thought you said you did not know anything about politics. Now what about Cambodia? Is the Cambodian issue not politics?'

She just continued, 'But really, they are treating us like people in Cambodia, and that we are not going to tolerate,' and went on from there.

The following morning, very early in the morning, about half past five, they unlocked my cell. I had to prepare myself, I was moving again. I questioned them, 'What? Where to?' but they said it was not for them to tell me.

I went to have a shower. After bathing, I said, 'You know I cannot just go without saying goodbye to my comrades. I must just let them know that I am leaving this place, that I am being transferred.'

So I went from one cell to another, saying goodbye to the comrades. The staff grew angry; they did not want me to do that, but they could not prevent me. I was absolutely adamant. I intended to say goodbye. They were not going to stop me from doing that.

We all felt the pain, now that one more comrade was going away. Before that, they had taken Feziwe away. Life is hard. Even if we had not been staying together, hearing a comrade's voice can be really important. It builds you up. Those apartheid gods were once more trying their hardest to keep us from being happy together.

So they took me to Klerksdorp Prison.

Fourteen

Travelling from one prison to the other, I became pressed. I told them, 'Hey, I want to go to the loo.' They were reluctant. I was in the back of a van. I made it a showcase that they had to listen to me – I did not see any reason why they should stop me from going to the loo, for sure. Eventually they stopped at Potchefstroom police station, to let me use the toilet.

Potchefstroom was where the system first arrested me. Now here I was, and coming back like this. Knowing that I was left with only a few months – oh, nearly 12 months out of the 60-month sentence. Other memories, too – most of my family, both maternal and paternal, live at Potchefstroom. I returned to the van, to go on to Klerksdorp Prison.

And when I got there, guess what happened. I was taken to the isolation section, straightaway. I met a warrant officer, the man who was head of that particular prison, Braun, and Sergeant Coetsee, Sergeant Sibusi, and a Mrs Kotze. As usual, I was put in a single cell. I was puzzled because there were no comrades here at all. Instead they put me in a section with another two women, two common-law prisoners. We were in single cells after the evening lock-up, but we could move around, socialise with each other, during the day.

I turned to the wardresses: 'You told me I was out of segregation. What is happening?'

They replied, 'We were told that there was a person coming, and that she was from Pretoria Prison. So we don't know. We were told that we had to deal with this person and that is that.'

I automatically grew suspicious. It seemed likely that these characters intended to use those two women, the common-law prisoners, staying in that section against me. They do that type of thing often in prison, putting ordinary prisoners in with you to spy on you. I made it a showcase that these prisoners would go back to them empty handed.

There was one woman from Stillfontein, Lydia; another from

111

Mafikeng, Elizabeth. They seemed frightened when they saw me. I discovered later that they had been told a lot of stories about me – that I was moody, I liked fighting , I would be hostile, that I could attack them at any time, for no reason at all. Not surprisingly, I did not get along with them very well at first. But in time I succeeded in building up trust with them.

Neither of them had any money for extras. By that time I was allowed to buy toiletries. I told them, 'Hey, come here. I've got toiletries here. And I believe in sharing. So let's share all this.'

We shared out the soap, creams, all that, even my Christmas sweets. I was practising the Freedom Charter, not only theorising about it: 'The people shall share in the country's wealth', even if at that point it was only the section's wealth.

That put something into them. Here was a character about whom they had been given false information, a character who turned out completely differently to what they had been told. Sorry!

Yet again we confronted this issue that they served us different food – because they claimed that common-law prisoners had to eat trash. I was determined that definitely, uh huh, this was not going to affect our relations. So I complained. Immediately we got the same diet. It was nice. They were willing to treat other people badly; but they had discovered, at last, that I was going to say 'Stop this.'

Elizabeth had been convicted for *dagga*, Lydia was serving a long period for theft. She had stolen money from where she was working.

And they had very different backgrounds. Elizabeth Mashangu was a married woman with three sons. One son was working in Rustenburg in the mines, the others were attending school in Mafikeng. She was miserable; she got no visits, no letters. And in prison that is frustrating; you begin to think your people have decided to disassociate themselves from you. I think this breaks up many marriages. We look at the saying that a friend in need is a friend indeed. If your husband fails to be on your side while you are in prison, it can only hurt.

Lydia did at least get visits from her people. Although they were not frequent, at least her people came. She got letters, she knew about what was happening in her family.

I took it to be my duty as a revolutionary to build these two characters. Of course: they are my people, I had to be with them. I used to call Elizabeth 'Mama'; she was a mother in any case, older

112

than the rest of us. And she was pleased to be called Mama. You have to learn tactics, you have to study how to make a person know she has a place in this life.

Elizabeth was a complete illiterate. When she came into prison she made a cross; she could not write her name. She could not read. I told her, 'I intend to teach you how to write. I know that you were never in a position to learn how to write, and I understand that. That is the reason some of us are here, because of our dissatisfaction with those who refused to teach us how to write.' And I made it my responsibility to teach her.

I gave her the basics, teaching her the alphabet. I realised, then, that she was a brilliant person. She could count immediately. I used to sit with her for hours – she would insist. She would just call me, a young girl like me: 'Kona, come here. How do you pronounce this word?' And she would spell it out, after she had understood the alphabet. 'Now how do you say this, how do you do this?' She was so eager to know, it gave me the power to teach her.

I stayed with her from October 1981 to May 1982, and believe you me, when she left she could write her name, her surname, all of her kids' names; she could even write a letter.

She was so grateful. But I told her, 'No, this is my duty. I cannot just leave you because we are from different places. You are my mother, my person, we belong to the same nation. It is up to me to see to it that wherever I go I have to educate people.'

Mama Lydia used to smoke. I made sure that I bought her matches. Every Friday all prisoners received a ration of cigarettes. I got 30 cigarettes. I made sure that I gave my cigarettes to Mama Lydia. She felt at home; she admitted, 'I don't know, but it seems you are a godsend.' I told Elizabeth that she also had to donate her ration; we lived as a family, one family, united.

Because my actions went hand in hand with my words, that peculiar picture they had of me completely vanished. And we succeeded in defeating the enemy, who had thought that they could use these two women as informers. In fact I was in a position to turn these women to the people's side.

The prison staff began to think, 'Uh huh, this person is really successful in winning over these prisoners.' Elizabeth and Lydia used to come back and tell me what happened: they would go for breakfast in the morning, or for lunch or supper, to collect the food from the kitchen. While they were fetching the food the wardresses would ask them what I had said to them, and all that. But I never talked explicit politics with them, ever. Eventually the staff had to admit that I was playing it safe, even winning the confidence of these people.

Mama Elizabeth ironed during the day; they gave her a lot of ironing. We were living on the first floor, with an exercise yard on the second floor. There was a wall up there, a big wall, with a washing line on it. They would hold their church services there sometimes.

The Prisons Department brought two sewing machines. The work was meant for these two women; I had made it totally clear to them: 'You know I told them in the other prisons that I will not work, and this is what I will repeat to you. I will not work.' Lydia was particularly good at sewing, and she did a lot. They used to bring clothes for her to sew, sometimes to mend. I was just looking at them work, doing precisely nothing. I would wash my clothes and iron them myself.

Then I decided to bring the spirit of harmony further into the lives of these two people. Because of my resistance in other prisons, the wardresses did not even try to make me clean the prison. These other two were given the work instead. So I sat down with the two of them and we discussed the cleaning of the section.

They reacted: 'No, we are supposed to do the cleaning; you are not supposed to do that.'

I persisted: 'Listen, I am not going to agree to that. Although you were told that you should do all the cleaning, I think this would be unfair on my part. The section where I am staying I will clean, and I am going to help you in cleaning the section's passage and stairs. Although with the other work, forget it! I won't help you with that.' For instance they told us the courtyard on the second floor had to be brushed, scrubbed and polished. I made it clear, 'Eh, these people. Who's supposed to do all this work? I won't do it.' And I didn't.

Poor Mama Elizabeth and Lydia did that work. Sometimes they would bring other prisoners to help. Mama Elizabeth and Lydia would work on the passage, just on the passage, and the other prisoners would scrub the floors of the courtyard and the wall, and do it properly.

I fell ill. I had tonsilitis. I always liked singing, but after singing for some time the tonsils would start up. I became so ill I could not even talk. I felt miserably depressed. In December the doctor decided I had to have an operation. They planned it for 26 December.

On Christmas morning I was taken to Klerksdorp Hospital, very early in the morning. A 'white' hospital – you know we have this illness in South Africa, this disease with black hospitals, white hospitals, coloured hospitals. They took me to a white hospital, rushed me in. I saw some of the cleaners, the black cleaners there, but they refused to speak to me. Some of them already knew that any black people who are taken to that place must be prisoners. So they got anxious. And I, I was too sick, too angry because I could not even eat my Christmas sweets.

They bundled me into the theatre, made me unconscious, operated on me. And I came back to the prison the same day, bleeding badly. They stuck me in my cell, they informed me that anyway I had Mama Lydia and Mama Elizabeth to look after me in the night, even though they were in separate cells; if there was anything I needed I could always ring the bell.

On 31 December I grew desperate. They gave me their medicine but the pains were unbearable. In the middle of the night I rang the bell. Lydia and Elizabeth, they shouted, called these people, rang their bells too. Nobody came. Ringing, shouting, and nobody came at all.

The next morning I was just furious. The people who were on night duty merely commented that they did not hear the bell. It had to be a deliberate ploy.

It took time for me to be fully cured. It took time before I could hear properly. I could not eat for days; I could only swallow porridge, thinned down. It is not nice, being ill like that in prison.

Luckily, by then I had established a very good friendship with these two women; they were nice people. Later we were joined by a certain coloured prisoner – I forget her name, maybe I have a reason for forgetting her name. When she arrived I suspected that these women were not giving the wardresses enough information about me. And really, that person made it very clear that she was there to spy. Unfortunately for her she found nothing to offer.

She was arrogant, a bully; she had this idea that because she was coloured she had to be treated better than the other people around her – and this was something which we had eliminated amongst ourselves. We were all prisoners; we believed we should have equal treatment. Therefore, she could not dominate like she thought she should. There was a close-knitted friendship between the three of us; when she came in with all her arrogance, she came as an intruder. We offered her nothing.

In Klerksdorp, one night, I think it was about one or two, hey! we heard men screaming, crying, being seriously beaten up.

Klerksdorp prison is just one building, divided into a women's section and a men's section. Even though the men were segregated from us, they were not far away. In prison there are gangsters: they have names like The Twenty-Eights, The Big Fives, The Twenty-Seven. In the cells, these gangs work. That day they had been left together. They started playing dice in the cells and I understand the fighting started there. The warders in charge failed to control them, so they called in all of the prison warders, all. Jesus. Those men were seriously beaten. Grown up men, screaming 'mama, mama!' It went on for hours.

The following day many of them were taken to hospital with major injuries.

In December, during the night in the early hours, a siren went off. Usually in prison they don't ring the siren at night without a purpose. They had found that two prisoners who were working in the kitchen, two men, had run away. It appears it had all been properly planned. The security of the place was weaker at that time, and these men had studied it thoroughly. When the staff realised that the number of prisoners had decreased, they looked all over the place, failed to find the men, set off the siren – hey, there was a lot of movement in the prison that night. And when I left prison those two men had not been re-arrested.

Many male prisoners succeeded in escaping from Klerksdorp. In fact, while they were out searching for these two who had run away, they found some other men who had escaped from the prison some months earlier. But those two they could not find.

They put a white woman in a cell just beneath mine. She was a hobo, arrested for drunkenness. She was so dirty it was unbelievable. These characters do have this one disadvantage: if one whitey happens to be poor, the others do not want to associate themselves with him or her. I am not a racist, but you can see that happen. If you are familiar with South Africa, you know that if a person is black that person is suffering. It is not significant to say that a certain black person is poor because the majority of blacks are poor. And there is this thing among blacks, that we have to try to help each other; if we do not help each other no one else is going to help us, that is for sure.

But white South Africans are brought up with the idea that whites must be superior. So failing to maintain that superiority is an affront, the others don't want to know about it. The person concerned just collapses, mentally and otherwise.

So this poor woman appeared seriously affected, drinking spirits

116

and that. Even so, when she came into prison she got treated like a queen compared to the rest of us.

In Klerksdorp Prison, unlike Pretoria Prison, most of the convicted prisoners were arrested for pass-law violations. In that year the Klerksdorp police arrested as many as 29,000 people, just on pass-law offences alone. Honestly, the number of people arrested was high, almost incredible.

Klerksdorp is where most of the mines are. Many of the largest mines in South Africa are around that area, concentrated there. The mines use migrant workers. And apartheid forces these miners to leave their families, to come to the cities, to the mines for work, without their wives and children. The families remain in the 'homelands' – where there is a lot of starvation, with insufficient land and drought. These women and children have absolutely nothing unless the man sends something back to them. You find that after a time some of these migrant workers no longer send anything to their families. The women have no choice: they have to follow their husbands to the mines. Around this area, we have people from Lesotho, Transkei, Ciskei, Qwaqwa, Bophuthatswana, Natal, Mozambique, Malawi, Botswana; you name it, they are there. It is the maelstrom of the mining industry, that place. These women are required by law to have passes to stay in that area, and, of course, they don't have. So they end up in prison for pass-law offences.

The situation is heartbreaking. There are whites owning farms around that area. There is one farmer called Napy; he is one of those whites who takes advantage of the plight of blacks, of black women – women who are there because of the suffering, because of the starvation in the homelands; who do not have reference books; who only regret that they do not qualify to remain in the urban area; who are permitted by law to stay only in the homelands and watch their children die of hunger. This man profits from their plight.

Napy has a farm, a big farm where he has built houses. He rents out these houses. Certain people work for him just to get accommodation and food, no wage. These women know Napy exploits them, but they can do nothing, because they are still illegal immigrants. The police know about that farm, and let him keep these women there, exploited and illegal as they are. But what else can these women do?

These women come to the mines following their husbands. Some come not because their husbands are there, but because they have

117

decided to turn to prostitution. Prostitution is rife in that area, with all the men working there without families. These women do not have accommodation; some of them have been chased out by this Napy, some have no place to sleep at all.

That place, Klerksdorp. It was the first time in my life that I heard that a person can sleep in a tree, with a baby on her back. It is happening, it is a practical thing to do, it is happening in our South Africa, in Klerksdorp at the mines. Not once, not twice, but regularly. And the only cause, the sole reason for that misery, is apartheid.

The police would raid the surrounding areas, arrest a lot of these mothers, together with their kids. My cell was near the entrance gate, the main entrance. Every Monday afternoon I could hear them open the door. You would hear a lot of noise – kids crying, mothers bundled into the reception offices. These characters do not see anything wrong in that; they call it normal.

But we cannot call it normal. This system is sick. People are sleeping in ditches, sleeping in trees in their own country, their own motherland. The people's document, the Freedom Charter, proclaims: 'There shall be houses, security and comfort'. Where is the security? Where is the comfort today? This evil system has made our lives a pitiful thing. And until South Africa is in the hands of the people, not the minority, nothing will come right. Until the people shall govern our people will still be sleeping in ditches, in trees. It is for the people of South Africa to remove all these terrible things. It is our duty.

Most of the convicts at Klerksdorp Prison, as I have said, are there for pass-law offences. Sometimes you find the father is in prison, arrested under the pass laws; the mother, together with the kids, all in prison for pass laws. There are certain families where prison is normal life; some of these people have spent most of their lives in prison for pass laws. And we tell them we must devise means of getting rid of these pass laws. We did not create them; I don't see any reason why we should abide by the laws we did not make.

Klerksdorp Prison teaches you to feel the weight of apartheid. Here there are people who hold up the economy of the country, having left their families to make Anglo-American rich, to turn the Harry Oppenheimers, *them*, into millionaires. And the people are suffering. The workers have nothing. It is for these workers to say: 'Oppenheimers, we have had enough. We have made you rich enough; now we have to take the mines. We must use our country's wealth to create a place where we can all live like human beings, not animals.' It is for the workers to stand up.

We know that the big businessmen, the apartheid gods, will fight to the last man to preserve their profits. But it is for us to say victory is certain. *A luta.*

At Klerksdorp I was just passing the time until my release. Of course, I continued with my complaints, making it explicitly clear to them that I wouldn't stop protesting against their rules and regulations. It is better, it is part of being human, to know the difference beween right and wrong. And they are wrong. So a person has to tell them. 'You are wrong. And I am not going to accept that.' You have to be able to say no.

Klerksdorp Prison was really monotonous, compared to Pretoria. Pretoria, man, although we were behind bars, there was life. You could make something out of the nothing they permitted you. There were comrades there. But at Klerksdorp life was boring. You had singing, and the minor distractions of bathing, washing, cleaning the place.

I encountered various problems at Klerksdorp, but they were all relatively minor. When a problem came up, I would raise it, tell them I didn't like one two three. And in most cases, unlike in the other prisons, they would attend to the problems. So life was not a list of one fight after another. They were reasonable.

I got a visit from Brigadier Venter. I complained that I wanted to be taken to my other comrades. He explained that the Commissioner of Prisons had taken a decision that I was not to stay with the comrades, since I was responsible for most of the disturbances inside prison. They saw me as a threat.

I got another visit from Brigadier Van Zyl. I pushed him, 'Until today I am waiting for my clothes. I am aware that the other prisoners are wearing their own clothes now, not the uniform – what about me?' He replied, 'You are joking, we are not going to give you the clothes. We are not going to make it easy for you, to let you think you have defeated us. When you come back to prison – because you won't last outside, we are going to come and pick you up again – you can wear your clothes then. But not now.'

And they did not give me my own clothes until my release. But I was very happy, because we did achieve so much, real achievements, in our fights inside. We won those fights. It took time, it took struggle, it took suffering. But we did succeed, and that was because comrades were fighting. When I came to Kroonstad Prison, I found a bed with sheets, pillows, all that; because other comrades like Mama Dorothy and Mama Aminah had fought from the beginning. We made them change the clothes, change the food. I rejoice that most of my comrades were now putting on their clothes. They had been forced to give us equality in some things – although the struggle is not yet complete, we advance step by step. Compared to the life we got when we entered prison, we won major victories.

I was released on 26 October 1982. A week before I wrote a letter to my people telling them to come and fetch me, I did not want to be transported in the prison truck. On the Tuesday my brother and sister-in-law fetched me. There was jubilation in my family to see me back home. My son, whom I'd left when he was five was now 11 years, a big boy. Thanks to my loving Mum, my family and good friends for looking after him during my absence. My family and comrades organised a welcome party for me. It was a warm welcome.

Seeing my people again, standing outside, feeling welcomed, and my comrades all there, I knew I had come home again.

Postscript

Umzima, mchana, umzima. The struggle is hard and long. Today I sit in a small room, with white walls, a tiny bed, a table there. At least I can open the door when I want to. The rulers of this country have declared a State of Emergency. We heard that my name had appeared on the death squad hit list, so it would not just be arrest and detention this time. So I live for a while in a little white barren room in another town, and then I move on. I cannot walk into the city centre, in this different city, for fear someone will recognise me. I change hats, *doeks*, make-up, hair styles. It has become a game. My comrades take care of me. So many of us these days are 'swimming'. We hide like fish in the water, one person among the people, my people.

We learned some lessons in their prisons. They thought they could attack us: they failed. We first learned that we could win against them. Even with nothing; even with only our hands and our

120

comradeship and our determination, we could defeat them. We have faced their viciousness before and won.

It is not an easy walk, this path we chose – but then you have to look at how we live in our country today. Our people know starvation, pain, broken families, broken lives. Our existence is such a misery when we succumb, when we accept their evil system, when we live just as they intend us to live, in the bantustans in the townships. They have left us no alternative but to fight.

We know what we want. Ours is a just struggle – the people shall govern. We have learned to share, here we have nothing; we have learned to build each other up, to give each other strength. We know our demands – the Freedom Charter demands. We know what we must do to live above all as human beings. Our future South Africa is being hammered out in our struggle today.

They have never learned. They still think they can show us an iron hand. They have declared a State of Emergency, and I am here in this small room. But they should know by now that we are not going to succumb. They send their troops to shoot us, their hit squads to shoot us, they have thrown us into the fire with their oppression. The people's resistance is turning into steel. War with no surrender. We rely upon our comrades, upon ourselves, upon our people. We stand united. They have thrown thousands into prisons since they declared the State of Emergency. The papers report 200 detainees at Pollsmoor Prison go on hunger strike, 400 at John Vorster Square, 200 at Johannesburg Prison. The courage of the people, the strength of the masses, never ends, and they failed to break me alone. Where are they going to land?

They could not stop our determination that one day liberation shall come, that victory is certain. We know it now, we feel it in the streets, the bloody streets; we shall take the country and give it to the people, where it belongs. When I came out I said we were going to do it, and we are doing it now. The people are on the march.

Since my release from prison, I have put my shoulder to the wheel. The people are organising. At rallies, at meetings, at night vigils for fallen comrades, I have often asked: 'As mothers, can we let our children die for us? Let them die fighting the beast, die fighting the apartheid monster which makes our lives a tale of broken hearts? Can we, as mothers, not take the fight to the enemy? Can *we* not stand up and be counted?'

The pace is changing, the world is changing around us. We are making it change. We are on the offensive. *A luta continua*. Victory is certain.